# PROCRASTINATION

GUIDE TO THE PSYCHOLOGY OF
MOTIVATION.
BEAT YOUR ADDICTIONS & BAD
HABITS, DESTROY AND OVERCOME
LAZINESS, CURE YOUR MIND AND
BECOME PRODUCTIVE

**SCOTT BRAIN**

# Table Of Contents

# Introduction

Procrastination is a tough thing to understand which is impressive considering that the definition is so simple. Procrastination is when you delay or postpone something that needs to be done. There are many different reasons why people do this and it's something that we're going to be covering in depth in this guidebook so that you can learn how to avoid it and recognize signs in yourself about why and how you do it. One of the most common reasons for procrastination are simply because you don't want to do something. A great example to get you to understand a little bit more about what we mean, is if you have a goal to clean your house within an hour, you're probably not going to want to do it for two reasons. One, because you have a rigid timeline and two, because it's not fun to clean your house. If you're a teenager, you'd much rather play video games. If you're an adult you probably much rather be watching social media or relaxing instead of having to clean after you've just gotten off of work. Or if you have to clean before you're going to work. If you have children this is doubly so because you don't want to be cleaning while you have to watch your children and you would instead be spending time with your children. This shows us that the biggest reason that people procrastinate is simply because they don't want to do something.

Procrastination also has a stigma attached to it. People assume that if you're a procrastinator it is merely because you don't have the will power to force yourself to do things or your lazy. This is a statement made in ignorance. This doesn't mean stupid. It just means that they don't know about this and there speaking without knowledge. It's a much more severe situation than what they think. When you're faced with the decision or a task that you need to complete, we usually rely on our self-control to push ourselves to get things done. That part is correct. Our motivation is based on expectation of receiving some kind of reward for our effort and that can also support self-control and make it more likely that we will get things done.

However, what people don't take into account is the fact that there are various de-motivating factors that we can experience throughout our day and throughout our lives which have the opposite effect on our motivation. That makes it more likely that we're going to procrastinate. Anxiety and fear of failing are two significant factors that can cause us to delay things unnecessarily, especially when we're given a task that is unpleasant.

People tend to want to procrastinate more if they've noticed that a reward is too far in the future. We tend to want instant gratification, which means we want our reward now. We don't want to have to wait for it and if the reward is far in the future, it tends to get discounted. When we're trying to do something, we don't want to do, it is easier to do something that you don't want to do when you know you're going to get a reward immediately after. It becomes harder if that reward is months or years into the future.

Fear is another big reason people procrastinate as we've said before and to be able to stop the procrastination you will have to be able to stop being afraid. If you are easily distracted then that's a big reason people procrastinate as well. We live in an age that is obsessed with technology and we are glued to our phones every second of the day. This makes it very much more challenging to stay focused on the tasks at hand or really on any task in general.

Procrastination may have a genetic component to it. Several studies have been debating the origin of procrastination and one study found that procrastination could be a byproduct of impulsivity and it could be heritable. This is due to both sharing a great deal of genetic variation and they have an essential aspect of a shared variability in goal management.

Even if this is true and you have a predisposition to procrastination it doesn't mean you can't do something about it to fix it. You don't have to stay in this situation. You can choose to get yourself out and beat this issue.

You could be affecting other's workload when you procrastinate, and nobody likes having a dumped work that another employee fails to do. If you're working in a career field where you work with other people (which is many people in the population excluding people that work at home as mostly they would just be working with themselves). It sets the stage for feelings of anxiety and resentments in the people you work with because you haven't been able to finish tasks or took too long to do so. If you work at a company and you're piling work on for other people because you're procrastinating and unable to finish it yourself your coworkers may also think you shouldn't work with them.

Procrastination can cause actual pain. Studies have shown that when we procrastinate about things that make us uncomfortable, medical imaging has been able to show that people can feel pain. The pain that centers in the brain tend to light up when contemplating on working on something that makes them uncomfortable. Like math for an example. Our natural reaction when we're confronted with pain is avoidance. This is one reason why people procrastinate so much. Specific tasks make us feel inadequate so in order to avoid feeling like that we just don't do it. In real life a lot of this is happening subconsciously but it still fixable and you don't have to keep with this space.

Procrastinators care too much not too little. The fact of the matter is they are far from being carefree and they tend to worry just as much, if not more than other people. The typical procrastinator worries that they're not good enough or that people are going to judge them or even that they will get disapproved, ridiculed or made fun of. Whatever the patterns of the feelings behind it, procrastinators worry a lot so it's not a matter of them not caring at all, it's a matter of them caring too much.

Studies have also shown that procrastination is affected by fatigue. In fact, researchers have shown that the number one reason people procrastinate is fatigue. This makes a lot of sense because when we are tired, we're low on energy and when overcoming our tendencies of procrastination, we need energy to do it. If we don't have any energy to speak of then we're setting ourselves up for failure.

If we don't have any energy left procrastination arises simply because we're too tired to get anything done.

Waiting for tomorrow isn't going to help you either. You're not going to feel any better about it tomorrow than you do now. Holding out for a better day then isn't going to work because you're not going to want to do it anymore just because the timing is different. It's just your mind trying to play tricks on you to make you think that you will. Every time we say maybe I will feel more like it tomorrow; it just illustrates that we feel that we are not very good at it right now and that we might feel happy if we try again tomorrow.

The problem is that your too focused on your current situation and how you're feeling right now. We tend to assume that how we're feeling now is how we're going to feel in a future setting. The trouble is that you should do it now so that you can get it over with. Your affective state is positive but you're irrationally forecasting how you feel today is the same as you how you're going to feel the next day. On the next day you're still faced with a task that you don't like. Therefore, your thoughts are the same and you still feel just as anxious and frustrated and you don't feel any better about it.

This forces you to have a decision. Should you give in and procrastinate again, or should you do the right thing and just get it over with, so you won't have to worry about it or stress anymore. We aim to look to tomorrow – not with dread, but with newfound excitement and curiosity. The tips can continue to be used as helpful tools, keeping us in a today mindset.

We aim to consider the long-term implications of our actions better, and the profound impact they can have on our own lives, as well as the lives of those around us. By doing this, we also aim to decrease the overall amount of stress and anxiety that we live with.

We aim to look our obligations in the eye and stop pretending that our neglect of them is a harmless habit. We aim to force the first few starter steps – to do a little, even if we can't do a lot. We aim to pass up on the instant gratification that keeps us from experiencing long-term peace, joy, and success.

We aim to gain and retain momentum – in our actions and in our attitudes. To stay motivated, take breaks as we need to, and to make time for those things that make us feel refreshed and recharged.

We aim to be more productive – personally and professionally. We aim to become leaders – for ourselves and for those around us. We aim to accept the fact that life rarely works according to our plans. It follows its own rules; not ours.

We aim to make the most of the present moment, which is the only moment we have. To embrace the opportunities we have, and to realize they may never come again. We aim to stop waiting for a better moment, for an excuse, or for inspiration in order to act. We aim to keep in mind that what's difficult now will be just as tricky later.

In short, we aim to stop saying... tomorrow works better. tomorrow.

To learn how that is done, let's spend a little more time talking about procrastination and what it is.

## CHAPTER 1

# Procrastination and Laziness

**M**any people mistake procrastination for laziness, yet they are very unique. Laziness is a dormant procedure while procrastinating is a functioning procedure. Procrastination includes deciding to accomplish something less significant rather than the pivotal undertaking while apathy is inertia, failure to act or reluctance to make a move. Most procrastinators have a bustling existence. They are always occupied with agreeable and straightforward errands instead of apparently extreme occupations that are progressively significant or fulfilling.

Though they are different from each other but one thing that procrastination and laziness do have in common is that there is zero motivation. Your procrastinating self-differs from your lazy self in that you do plan to finish the task at hand, and more often than not, you do finish — even though it means you have to deal with a lot of headaches in the process since you wasted precious time.

The huge outcome of delaying isn't the lost time that you could have utilized on beneficial activities yet the blame and disgrace that accompanies realizing that you are stalling. At the point when you tarry, you feel terrible about it. On the off chance that you stall for quite a while, you feel demotivated. In extraordinary cases, procrastination causes an absence of center throughout everyday life. It prompts despondency, work misfortune, and bombed vocations.

Laziness and procrastination can affect your life. The explanations behind tarrying may fluctuate starting with one individual then onto the next, yet the results of the negative propensities are comparative. You most likely tarry as a result of concealed feelings of trepidation, stress, absence of inspiration, or different reasons. Whatever the reasons, you have to make a move at the earliest opportunity since lethargy and procrastination have an all the more harming sway that you most likely think. Here is the means by which they decimate your life.

## Losing valuable time

Your life is estimated by time. What amount of your life have you squandered by putting off that significant assignment till tomorrow or the day after tomorrow? You can envision how much time you lose by not making a move. You will acknowledge later that you are 10 years more established, yet you have not accomplished your objectives since you procrastinated.

## Passing up on brilliant chances

What number of chances for development have you missed in light of the fact that you didn't act? This may make you need to kick yourself. We have all missed essential gatherings, business arrangements, excursions, and learning openings in light of apathy or dawdling.

What you would prefer not to recognize is that the open door could have transformed you. Lamentably, dazzling possibilities are uncommon. They state Christmas comes however once every year. You are never guaranteed of another opportunity. Lingering and apathy grab openings from you and make you hopeless.

## Broken dreams

On the off chance that you don't make a move presently, nothing will change! The information and the craving to accomplish will take you no place in the event that you don't make a move. In the event that you need to accomplish wellness objectives, make the primary intense stride. Pay exercise center membership and begin working out. In case you're going to begin a business, explore, accumulate assets and build up your first outlet.

Have you at any point wound up asking why you can't accomplish something you need to do so ineffectively? You have to investigate the explanations for your activities. The odds are that you are lazy or procrastinating. We as a whole need an incredible future and have dreams of what we need to accomplish. It is the best way to have a superior life and appreciate our rewards for so much hard work. On the off chance that you are languid, you will lament the lost time and broken dreams that you never really accomplish.

Destroying your profession

In most vocation openings, your work influences the outcomes and decides your profession development. Stalling will make you miss cutoff times, neglect to make deals, or miss significant gatherings. Despite the fact that you may pull off it and hold your activity, you won't meet your week after week, month to month, or yearly targets. Your manager won't be satisfied with you and you will without a doubt pass up advancements and profession improvement openings. More terrible than that, you could lose your employment and ruin your vocation altogether. You can take a stab at concealing laziness and procrastinating for some time, however the results.

Confidence issues

Now and then low confidence makes us delay significant undertakings that could transform ourselves for better. However, what you have to acknowledge is that lingering intensifies the circumstance. Making a remarkable stride gives you certainty and motivates you to achieve your objectives.

At the point when you are in question, don't stop for a second; make a stride towards your objective. In the event that you sit tight for a really long time, you will bring down your confidence and obliterate your life. At the point when you have regard issues, you will pass up different chances and feel substandard before your equivalents. You may wind up feeling less important, and your activities could disrupt your life. Concentrate on building confidence. Rather than accepting that you can accomplish something, venture out, evacuate all questions.

Settling on an inappropriate decision

Lazy individuals regularly settle on an inappropriate choice. Why? They don't set aside some effort to investigate or examine the real factors before settling on the choice. On the off chance that you are lethargic, and you need to pick between finishing a particular undertaking today and acquiring a reward or finishing it later on and missing the reward, you will most likely settle on the last mentioned.

Individuals who tarry likewise have a similar issue. They put off complex dynamic procedures until they have a ton to break down and too brief period to do it viably. They experience the weight and wind up settling on choices dependent on their feelings. Poor decisions lead to negative musings that influence our satisfaction and personal satisfaction.

## Blame and lament

At the point when you neglect to finish an assignment at the suitable time, you feel regretful and scared. Your trust in your capacities goes down, and you begin investing more energy lamenting as opposed to attempting to improve your life. You likewise don't feel right around the individuals who finished their undertakings on schedule and accomplished their objectives.

## Awful notoriety

No one needs somebody who doesn't convey. We as a whole aversion questionable individual who give void guarantees. Lingering and lethargy harm your notoriety impressively when the individuals around you find that you can't be trusted. The propensity becomes more grounded as you become accustomed to it. You no longer want to accomplish something in any event, when you bomb your companions and friends and family. Individuals will in the long run quit confiding in you with basic tasks and may pull back from you to let you tidy up the chaos. An awful notoriety will cause you to lose business bargains. You will lose companions and incredible open doors in view of dawdling.

## Unexpected frailty

Indeed! You heard it right. Apathy and delaying lead to medical problems related with pressure, tension, and despondency. Lingering makes you work under tension in the event that you need to fulfill the time constraints. It expands the force of pressure identified with a specific assignment and makes it challenging to meet desires. You lose trust in your capacity. Uneasiness and misery crop in, and we as a whole realize they are quiet executioners.

Also, apathy will make you skip exercises, and this will unfavorably influence your wellbeing.

Fortunately, you have the ability to conquer lethargy and delaying. I am here to assist you with solid ideas and approaches that will ensure results. Assume responsibility for your life and carry on with the life you had always wanted liberated from laziness and stalling.

Typical Signs That You Are Lazy

Most slackers and lazy individuals deny it. No one needs to be lethargic, even that old companion who invests the vast majority of the energy sitting idle. We as a whole need to show we are gainful, persevering and determined in our obligations. However, actually we are clutching negative behavior patterns that could destroy our lives.

Is it accurate to say that you are ever occupied with trivial undertakings? Do you invest the majority of your energy in online life? This could be lethargy in mask. You have to take care of these propensities before it is past the point of no return. I am here to support you. This guidebook is for you in the event that you do the accompanying things.

Buying such a large number of things

A languid individual need to purchase whatever appears to make life simple. Sadly, the more significant part of the things lazy individuals purchase is pointless and just assistance them to do essential undertakings. On the off chance that you end up purchasing numerous pointless items, you are lazy! Superfluous things lead to more apathy until you assume responsibility for your life and choose to change the circumstance.

Taking a break over and over again

Do you end up considering a break at regular intervals of doing truly straightforward assignments? You are just searching for time to get lazy. At the point when things heat up, and you need to finish a specific activity, you want to take a break in the event that you are a lazy individual.

Approximating significant things

Being lazy is fun from the start. You rapidly recognize another lethargic individual in the work environment and become companions in a split second. On the off chance that your companion can't set aside some effort to confirm fundamental subtleties or cross-check realities on the web, you are a lethargic individual. Why? You are companions since you share similar propensities. Laziness is explicit by and large.

Reassigning errands

Now and again appointing obligations is very significant in the event that you are a supervisor. Lazy individuals need to feel like supervisors always. Regardless of whether you are a business official, you should carry out specific responsibilities without anyone else.

# How Procrastination Makes You Unhappy

It will lower your self-esteem: When you cannot complete essential tasks on time and you know it was out of your neglect, you are likely to experience a decreased level of self-esteem. You lose belief and confidence in yourself, which automatically turns into a loss of happiness.

Lost opportunities: How many opportunities have you lost because of procrastination? Have you not seen your friends grab those same opportunities and succeed when you could not (maybe you have better skills?). One thing about opportunities is that they knock at your door only once. If seized, they may have improved your life; it feels terrible when you know you missed out because you procrastinated.

Damaged relationships: We have seen that when you don't do things in time, you will probably use a lie to explain yourself. Often, the liar is the only person believing the lies: other people do not buy it primarily if you use the same tactic repeatedly. This is how you lose friends. You will also damage your love relationship if you are always late for dates or when you keep postponing an important talk. Who would be happy without friends and on an unstable relationship?

Killing time: Time is one of the most valuable resources we have. If time just passes you by, you are at a disadvantage: important things will pass you by too. Unfortunately, procrastinators seem to place a significant emphasis on time, but they waste it and get mad when they realize they lost it. It is a terrible feeling when you cannot turn back the hands of time; when time goes, you lose it forever. You have to live with the feelings of regret and frustration with yourself.

# CHAPTER 2

# Addiction and Procrastination Two Sides of the Same Currency

Addiction and procrastination can coincide with each other.

Addiction is considered by many as a mental illness, though some argue that it is a moral failing. Regardless, addiction is mostly a choice. You choose to try out and experiment with a drug or activity, and you choose to continue using or doing it. You will decide whether to fear the addiction or to embrace it. Eventually, your condition will sink in and the long-term effects will be felt, though despite the consequences and the amount of help you get, discontinuation will still depend on your willingness to stop and change.

You could look up a handful of definitions for the term "addiction," but to keep things simple, it's a condition wherein a person finds it difficult or is unable to stop himself/herself from performing an activity or consuming a substance.

It should be noted that the term 'addiction' is different from 'misuse', as the latter is used to misdescribe the use of substances or without a prescription. That doesn't necessarily imply, though, that a person who misuses a substance will automatically get addicted to it.

Corresponding to procrastination, a habit of doing things later can be a mental illness in the latter as you're addicted to delaying or postponing something. On the other hand, you are delaying something vital because you have been doing something you have been addicted to than doing your task first.

Procrastination comes in many forms. For one, you could be investing too much time on the Internet. With the rise and the continued development of technology, it is unquestionable that procrastination through it has only become more prevalent, which is especially true for those who are fond of social media. In the middle of your creative process, you may also get distracted by quick mobile games and other information that comes from your screen. What starts as a short breather could end up becoming a powerful time consumer. We're not blaming technology and its development for your suffering; we're only saying that it can significantly impact your performance and attention span.

Have you ever been in a situation wherein you're just sitting in your room trying to study, then all of a sudden, a thought pops up: "Wow? Maybe this place sure could use some tidying up?" or maybe you wanted to go for a "quick" stroll around the park to "gather some inspiration." You're trying to prepare for something significant, but then in a flash, every tedious activity and chore your mother insists you to do just becomes an enriching task — but only for that exact moment. And have you ever wondered why these types of situations happen? We will cover all the bits and pieces of procrastination — what it is, how it is done, and how this simple act could ruin a lot of lives when allowed to continue.

Did you know that procrastination is closely linked to stress and anxiety? When you're feeling unproductive, this will result to feelings of guilt and depression, and when you start to feel so down in the dumps, your body wouldn't function the way you want it to, rendering you unable to move. Prolonged inactivity could also damage your posture and overall physical well-being because you don't get to exercise or even stretch properly. Besides, those all-nighters aren't particularly good for your health as you sacrifice your sleeping hours for additional work time. During those periods you would also take in some food and beverages that boost energy. Sure, we'll give those some credit for actually doing their job well, but those consumables just don't have enough nutrients for your always working self, and eventually, this will exhaust you of your remaining energy — this is why you feel so tired and gloomy after eating large amounts of caffeine.

As well as in laziness, both have different spelling, of course but they can also be similar at some point. Here's why:

Humans have long ago felt this undesirable trait but haven't considered it as one yet in the earliest of days. Our ancestors justified laziness as an act of survival and preserving their energies to be able to endure longer days without resources, compete for it when available, and fend off or flee from predators and their own enemies. Back in the early days, there wasn't much time to plan for the next move; instincts served as the only thing to help them with their judgement of the situation. With the

24

sensation of the instant rewards for their hard work, it is only right to savor the glory, continue the act of energy conservation and live to see another day.

The first people to reportedly adapt the concept of slothfulness were the Desert Fathers, monks who lived in solitude in Egypt during the 4th century A.D. Evagrius of Pontus described slothfulness (termed as acedia) as a demon that lived within the monks to resent the desert and their state of living. "He depicts for him the long course of his lifetime, while bringing the burdens of asceticism before his eyes."

Fast forward to the modern era, survival via fight or flight is no longer necessary, as we get to enjoy the luxuries of technological, scientific and medical advancements. Our enemies can no longer hurt as when they so desire, and resources are easily accessible. But why do we still feel laziness or inactivity?

The number one reason for feeling laziness is negative emotions such as fear and depression, but did you know that there are other causes for it? Here we shall tackle the different psychological reasons for inactivity.

1. Fear and Depression

As in procrastination, people can feel lazy and would not want to work on anything because they either fear the task itself or are afraid of what its outcome may be when done poorly. But how can depression be linked to laziness? When a person is drowning in negative thoughts and emotions, creativity and motivation are often blocked out of their system. It could also be that the person has already experienced rejection and received negative criticism for his/her craft, and the natural response to feeling emotional pain would be avoidance.

## 2. Tiredness

Working too hard can have its downside, as it would require a large amount of energy and mental capacity. Physical exhaustion can lead to poor performance both physically and mentally, and eventually to the shutdown of your system. And when you feel tired, you wouldn't want to do anything other than rest, right? However, lazy people expend their energies on unimportant activities and leave the important ones undone. Does this sound familiar?

## 3. Poor Health

Poor health could also be linked to tiredness and exhaustion. When you are not eating right, you are not getting the right nutrients from the food your intake. Food is considered to be a basic need for a self-evident reason: to increase energy and brain activity — two things that are needed to be able to function well. Note that a car needs gasoline or diesel to run. You wouldn't feed it some junk like butter or cooking oil and expect 100% efficiency, would you?

## 4. Lack of Motivation and Inspiration

When you feel like you're doing something without a purpose or without the proper compensation, you start to lose interest in being able actually to accomplish the task. And when that happens, you will always find reasons to stay away from it. In retrospect, there are those who choose not to get things done and find themselves to be a lot more stuck in awful situations, which makes them feel even more lazy and without a care in the world.

### 5. Poor Lifestyle

Nothing is more comforting than the feeling of going straight to bed after a long day. Often, we blame the nonliving thing for our lack of desire to move, claiming that we are dragged to it due to the significantly higher force of gravity it possesses. But is that really the cause? When we get too accustomed by the kind of pleasure a good rest brings to the table, we start to crave for more. And when things start to get out of control, that's when laziness kicks in.

### 6. Distractions

Maybe the newest version of a game has just been released, or the latest gossip in the world of social media is making huge waves. Whatever it may be, you just can't stop staring at or keep coming back to your phone to refresh it. What about that super important project? It's just lying there, accumulating dust and deprived of the attention it so desires.

## CHAPTER 3

# Inability to Make Decisions

Uncertainty is the most despised enemy of our capacity to make a move. It incapacitates us and makes it difficult to push ahead. Undertakings and activities are postponed until we figure out how to break out of the thought circle.

A lot of times we make up stories before we do whatever it is that needs to be done, stories that we believe is true and one the reinforce our inactions.

We make up stories in uncertainty before we make a decision, example if I eat, I will have the motivation to do the task, or maybe after I leave the gym, or I will get some rest and rip it up. Selling ourselves these lies that we know will hurt our productivity because of the uncertainty we have of the task ahead.

A lot of uncertainty comes from not knowing where to start, especially if the task seems overwhelming in chunk size. In cases where you have your home to clean up, doing the laundry or just doing some renovation to your home. These big tasks usually cause a lot of persons to procrastinate, just looking at the task and asking yourself, 'where do I even start'. Thinking that it would be much easier if you do it tomorrow or later or hiring out the task. And when we practice not to take immediate actions in these uncertainties, this then becomes a habit, and become embedded in our DNA. After which as I stated earlier is hard to break out of

All these uncertainties often stop us from growing evolving and be so much more than we currently are.

About each move we make is gone before by a decision between at least two alternatives. At the point when we go to these psychological crossroads, we think about the alternatives before us before pushing ahead. This is an appropriate and useful procedure. It encourages us to choose the choices that best commendation our objectives and conditions.

Be that as it may, a few people get trapped in a thought circle. They stall out at the thought stage. They never figure out how to pick between the alternatives before them. Their hesitation regularly makes them postpone making a move. In extreme cases, without an adequately convincing motivator to act - for instance, a manager undermining end - the postponement gets interminable.

Uncertainty can originate from numerous components, some of which we've just investigated.

For instance, an individual might be stressed that picking a sub-par choice will make the person in question be fruitless (dread of disappointment). He might be worried that picking ineffectively will constrain him to deliver defective work (compulsiveness). She may expect that making an inappropriate choice will produce unappealing outcomes (antipathy for chance).

Whatever its motivation, Procrastination consistently makes us progressively inclined to dawdling. We're bound to postpone making a move until we're sure that we're settling on the correct decisions. This quandary, obviously, can endure uncertainly.

I talk for a fact. I used to have incredible trouble picking between various choices. Here are two or three straightforward strategies I used to conquer this issue.

Individuals who can't settle on choices rapidly will in general experience dynamic irregularity. They frequently have various adaptations of themselves at various focuses for the duration of their lives. These adaptations speak to their dynamic selves right now.

Of course, if their inclinations don't adjust, there could be irregularities and flightiness factors.

For instance, an understudy may want for a test to be deferred with the goal that he may have more opportunity to contemplate. He may even be happy to do anything just to have it delayed for one more day.

This equivalent understudy, nonetheless, may feel diversely a couple of months before the test. Since there is a great deal of time to get ready, he may not feel any desperation to contemplate. He won't wish for the test to be delayed and he won't alarm at the measure of time left for him to plan.

This model shows a similar choice that is made in various circumstances. The facts demonstrate that choices can change just as be affected by current circumstances. Time irregularity is a type of dynamic irregularity. The aftereffects of choices can fundamentally influence the manner in which individuals think. Likewise, individuals can have various choices about their quick and faraway future.

We can all agree that deliberating, pondering weighing the pros and cons too much is not a form of decision making. Often these activities are used to replaced actual actions to make it appear as if something is being done. We experience this at work many times, meetings upon meetings are held over the same issue and no actually actions are taken. To avoid making tough decision that will affect or change a lot of outcomes, these choices are pondered over several times, before any actions are taken. Like filing for divorce from an abusive spouse emotionally and physically, resigning from a job to chase new opportunity, move to another city to do acting.

We will often deliberate over these tough decisions, but the issue in life is that we cannot live in two alternatives.

What we need to do is make a decision and then make that decision work, do our best to make sure the outcome of the choice you make is positive. Any time in life that we find ourselves deliberating too much about a decision too much, just make the choice and make the outcome of that decision the best.

## Step by Step Instructions to Overcome an Inability To Make Decisions

The most significant advance you can take to conquer Procrastination is to choose to settle on a choice. That is, focus on making a move, regardless of whether doing so implies accidentally picking the lesser of at least two alternatives.

Making a move short-circuits our motivation to hesitate as we trust that extra subtleties will settle on better choices. This is acceptable in light of the fact that we once in a while need more subtleties. Much of the time, we just persuade ourselves that we do so as to delay settling on a decision between contending choices. It's our method of managing apprehension and inconvenience about the obscure.

The significant thing to recollect is that this dread and inconvenience are once in a while justified. The actual expense of picking a not exactly perfect choice is typically unimportant. In the interim, the expense of permitting trepidation and uneasiness to deny us of our capacity to settle on choices is enormous; it attacks our profitability.

Notwithstanding making a promise to make a move even with vulnerability, it's imperative to become alright with settling on flawed choices.

This is a training I used to incredible impact in vanquishing my own Procrastination. I built up the propensity for asking myself, "What's the most terrible that can occur on the off chance that I pick an inappropriate choice?" In many cases, the most direct outcome imaginable wasn't awful in any way. Probably, it was just more negative than picking the perfect choice.

For instance, I would obsess about picking a café to have a social gathering with companions. Would it be a good idea for us to meet at a Mexican café? A Chinese eatery? A gourmet burger joint? I would overthink the choice and become incapacitated all the while. Normally, I'd stall the choice, regularly to the point that it got difficult to reserve a spot.

Eventually, the decision didn't make a difference. The most direct outcome imaginable was that we'd persevere through awful help or defective food. Yet, that was a hazard with the entirety of eateries. At long last, the main thing that really made a difference was that everybody in our gathering appreciated each other's conversation. We would have done so paying little mind to the scene.

Here's the takeaway: on the off chance that you battle with Procrastination, start making a move. Shut down the pondering stage. You'll see that whichever choice you pick; the result won't be close to as terrible as you would envision.

## CHAPTER 4

# Living and Working with Procrastinators

All companies and organizations have goals and objectives to meet within a specific timeframe. Therefore, to become a valuable asset within any organization, you must learn to manage your time efficiently. Rest assured that once you manage your time well, the result would reflect positively in your output within the organization you are working with. With a better ability to manage your time effectively, you will definitely stand out in distinction as you continue to gain more promotions.

Nowadays, one of the significant challenges faced by most organizations is the lack of standards in organizing work, generally, in managing time in particular. Most organizations are therefore focusing in trainings that enable their employees to manage their time correctly. The reason is that proper time management will go a long way to facilitate the work of all staff and equally make it more effective. It is apparent that everyone within an organization has 24 hours daily, whereas almost every employee produces different results. Well, the disparities in the output by different colleagues is to a greater extent the function of how each of them manages their time. Thus, within the context of an organization, time management can be described as the management of the results of labor. Moreover, the art of time management boils down to what task is performed and in what quantity within a particular timeframe.

When analyzing the problem of managing time within an organization, consultants often make a distinction between corporate and personal time management. The reason is that aside being paid to help a company achieve its goals, employees equally have their own personal goals and dreams. So basically, personal time management is connected to time management within an organization. A person who manages his time well, has his guidelines and knows what he wants from life is therefore more likely to manage his time well and equally be efficient at what he does within an organization. It also goes without saying that the loss of an employee's personal time is directly related to inefficiency.

Thus, the whole company could end up suffering from the disorganization of its individual employees.

An ideal organization or institution is therefore one that builds its goals, while taking into account the goals of its employees. Most employees are continuously striving hard to make compromises that are geared towards balancing corporate and personal time management, so it's just but natural for companies to also consider these employees who make endless sacrifices to see that the company achieves both its short and long run objectives. Nevertheless, an employee can only compromise by choosing the best option for coexistence based on his study and understanding of both corporate time management and personal time management.

## Procrastination and Time Management Within an Organization

Procrastination is a leading cause of time mismanagement within an organization, as many employees find ways to avoid a variety of tasks that need to be done. Unfortunately, this bad habit has a way of paralyzing and impacting efficiency negatively. There are actually many causes of procrastination within the corporate milieu and some of them include;

1) Inefficient planning

Most people who procrastinate are known to have poor time management skills. They always fail to plan and that explains why they end up either prioritizing the wrong things or failing even to prioritize at all. Remember that once you fail to plan your time efficiently, you are likely to postpone those tasks you consider tedious and difficult in favor of those you enjoy doing. Moreover, when specific tasks seem hard, procrastinators may have a low tolerance level. Similarly, they could equally feel overwhelmed when specific tasks seem too hard. In some instances, some employees may be reluctant to effectively plan on how to perform specific tasks simply because they feel marginalized for being the ones singled out to perform such tasks.

2) Multitasking

Multitasking equally has a way of making employees to procrastinate. This is particularly the case when employees perform many unrelated or unconnected tasks within an organization. Some employees are actually faced with many complicated and demanding workloads that they always find themselves foregoing some of the pertinent things that need to be handled. Thus, it is evident that many employees procrastinate and end up not using their working hours effectively because they are simply swamped to do everything at once. This therefore explains why it's of utmost importance for consultants to take into consideration the nature of jobs and how demanding they are before implementing time management policies.

3) Lack of clear goals

People who do not have clear goals are also likely to mismanage their time. This assertion can be explained by the fact that once you lack clear goals, you are more likely to spend more time on the wrong things. More so, if you haven't defined the amount of time allocated for each goal, it's easy to procrastinate, with the notion that there is no deadline you are trying to meet.

## 4) Problems with division of labor

In an organization setting where division of labor is not done correctly, it is easy for some personals to postpone specific essential tasks. This mainly happens when some employees are given a considerable workload, whereas others have very little to do. With a vast workload coupled with the pressure of trying to meet deadlines, some employees find themselves procrastinating, whereas some others find it extremely hard to manage their time effectively.

## 5) Distractions

Nowadays, many people spend their valuable work hours doing utterly useless stuff. For example, many employees spend a lot of their time browsing different social media sites, including Facebook, Instagram and Twitter, instead of concentrating on what they were paid to do. Recent studies have indicated that the average person spends about 5 years of his or her life on social media, and over two hours per day on social media. It is true that taking brief mental breaks throughout a workday helps in increasing individual productivity and performance, but of course, the downside is that you can quickly become addicted to specific social media sites.

## 6) Lack of self-discipline

Above all, some people procrastinate and end up mismanaging their working time because of lack of self-discipline or self-control. If you give yourself orders or instructions, but have a hard time following them, then you probably lack self-control. That said, even though the lack of self-discipline is not the primary cause of procrastination, it's known to be an essential factor.

## Implications of Poor Time Management

In the corporate world consultants are continuously working hard to design different strategies that are geared towards managing time effectively in the workplace. Poor time management is however known to result in adverse outcomes, some of which will be discussed in the subsequent paragraphs;

1) Poor productivity

If you want to be efficient in all your tasks, then you ought to manage your time wisely. The inability to plan your time well and stick to your goals simply translates to inefficiency. If you are faced with a massive workload at your office, an effective time management plan would be to complete related tasks together or sequentially. Nevertheless, the trick to be efficient and productive lies in planning ahead of time. Rest assured that when you plan ahead of time, you wouldn't be spending time jumping back and forth or backtracking specific tasks.

2) Poor quality work

There are no doubts that when you manage your time poorly in your workplace, it reflects in the quality of your output. The reality of the situation is that reduced time the executives causes typically the nature of your work to endure. This assertion can be explained by the fact that when you rush to complete a task at the last minute, you are likely to compromise its quality.

4) Wasted time

Poor management equally results in wasted time. It should be noted that time is always limited and once it's lost, it can never be regained. That said, you will definitely waste time if you spend many hours jumping from one social media platform to another or chatting with your friends while working on something important. You will only be distracting yourself and equally wasting time which could have been invested in something more valuable.

5) Loss of control

Above all, poor time management could result in loss of control over your life. It is evident that once you lost touch of what the next task is, you are likely to suffer from loss of control of your life. This can also result in anxiety as well as higher levels of stress, which can in turn affect your efficiency and productivity.

How organizations motivate employees to manage their time effectively

1) Extrinsic motivation

2) Goal based motivation

3) Intrinsic motivation

# Tips to Effectively Manage Your Time as an Employee Within the Corporate World

1) Set your goals correctly

One of the best ways of managing your time as an employee is to set the right goals that are measurable and achievable. That said, one of the best ways to set goals is to use the SMART method. In essence, you must set goals that are Specific, Measurable, Attainable, Relevant and equally Timely. Once this is done, you are likely to spend your time judiciously by trying to achieve your set goals within a specific timeframe.

2) Set a time limit to complete each task

Organizations typically go for employees who can effectively multitask. Nevertheless, most employees end up procrastinating and mismanaging time whenever they fail to set a time limit for a specific task or project. Well, the truth is that once you set a time constraint for a specific task, you become more focused and efficient. Moreover, in the process of allocating time for each task, you could as well identify potential problems and make plans for them before they even arise. Hence, you wouldn't need to spend valuable time trying to solve unforeseen problems.

3) Always prioritize wisely

Learning to prioritize wisely will equally help you manage your time better at your workplace. Remember that it would count for nothing if you make a schedule for various tasks, but fail to prioritize those ones which are more critical and urgent. As a matter of fact, you must distinguish between those tasks that are important and urgent, those that are important but not urgent, those that are urgent but not important and above all, those that are not urgent and not important. By so doing, you will learn to prioritize those things that need to be handled urgently.

4) Always plan ahead of time

Another tip of maximizing and making the best use of your time is by planning ahead of time. Always ensure that you begin each new day with a clear idea of what you need to do. That said, you should also make it a habit to always complete your daily tasks in order of importance and urgency. More so, at the end of each day, always remember to write your to-do-list for the next working day.

5) Organize yourself well

The importance of organizing yourself properly can never be overemphasized in time management. One of the best tools of self-organization is a calendar. You can always mark the deadline for projects or tasks that are an integral part of the overall project on your calendar. Of course, you should also think and determine the days that are best to perform specific tasks.

6) Take short breaks between tasks

Most often it becomes challenging to stay focused and motivated if we are doing so many tasks without a break. However, when you learn to take short breaks between tasks, you become more focused and efficient in whatever thing you are doing. That said, it is imperative always to allow some downtime between tasks so you can refresh yourself or even clear your head. During such short breaks, you can relax a little or even consume some of the things you enjoy.

## CHAPTER 5

# How to Build Mental Endurance and Self-Discipline

## Building Mental Toughness

You need to be mentally tough to squash and stomp out any doubts that may creep into your mind. Mental toughness is a valuable asset when it comes to overcoming your distractions and becoming a more self-disciplined person. Mentally tough people are not quitters. They have the drive to do what it takes to succeed; to get back up ten times after falling for nine.

A strong character is also essential for self-discipline. Often, a lack of self-discipline is a sign of weak character. Building a character will enable you to withstand any challenge you may face. If you are successful, self-discipline will never be a struggle in your life.

Here's a list on why you need mental toughness or endurance:

- Is required for managing emotions.
- Is required for controlling and handling your thoughts.
- Is the key to willpower.
- Is required to navigate through trying times.
- To establish a winner's mind
- Promotes longevity in your career or goals
- Allows you to handle distractions and keep your focus
- Teaches you to prioritize
- Teaches patience
- Gives you greater life satisfaction
- Allows you to reduce stress and anxiety

## How to Build Mental Toughness:

1. Develop a healthy support system

Create a positive, secure, and encouraging support system to gain strength from whenever required. During challenging times, we must be able to share our feelings with a close, trustworthy, and motivating group of people. Exchange thoughts and feelings, enlist the support of people you trust, learn about people's journey, gain constructive feedback, enlist support, and discuss possible alternatives. The people you surround yourself with contribute primarily to your thoughts and mental framework. Speaking to trusted people can help you gain new insights, views, and solutions about challenging situations, which in turn boosts your mental toughness.

2. Take cold showers

You might think this is unnecessary suffering, but it is not because taking cold showers has a lot of benefits such as boosting your immune system, increasing levels of testosterone, reducing inflammation, and so on. When the cold water touches your skin for the first time, try not to yell or wince. Just bear it and keep your mind and body as relaxed as possible by taking deep breaths. Try to stay in the cold water for at least 30 seconds and just make it longer as you get used to the coldness.

3. Minimize social media usage

It takes a lot of mental toughness to unplug from social media. You can either stop using it entirely or try to use it only when necessary, like for communication or sharing important stuff. But minimize social media usage as much as you can and just spend your free time doing more productive things. Believe it or not, Steve Jobs didn't let his kids use iPads because he knows how toxic it can get once people start to go online and use social media.

4. Get out of bed right away

When you hear your alarm go off in the morning, do not press the snooze button, and do not stay in your bed even for just one minute longer. Get out of bed right away and do something to keep your blood flowing. Splash your face with cold water, make coffee or tea, prepare breakfast, and just do anything to wake yourself up. This is all just mind over matter. And you will feel a lot better later on when you realize how much you were able to finish in a day because you woke up early.

5. Sleep on the floor

You can also try sleeping on the floor once in a while. You don't necessarily need to give up your comfortable bed for good. Just do this from time to time to help you build your mental toughness. For a really tough challenge, sleep without a blanket. Use a thin sheet if you are not ready for the difficulty level.

6. Do small exercises

This will not be your regular full-blown workout. That is another thing that you should be doing even if you are not trying to lose weight because it will keep your body strong and healthy. These mini workouts are workouts that you can incorporate in your everyday life.

7. Move slowly

You might think that this tip is counterintuitive, because slowness is often not associated with success and achieving goals. But this does not literally mean working at a slower pace. It just means that you do not make impulsive actions and snap decisions.

8. Get dirty

Some people are so afraid to get themselves dirty because getting dirty is way out of their comfort zone. Although being clean is something that we should all strive for, there is nothing wrong with getting yourself dirty from time to time.

9. Read

Reading a book can make you tougher mentally because it helps you improve your mental focus for an extended period of time. Read a book for a couple of hours every day; that can teach you a thing or two about delayed gratification, unlike television and online videos that are passive entertainment and do not really contribute anything to improving your mental toughness. Reading is also an activity that allows you to use your mind active and learn new information.

10. Take a break

When something doesn't help you achieve the desired results, go on a break or change your strategy rather than giving up. Tackle the task with a rejuvenated, fresher, and brand-new perspective after recharging your batteries. Real success and glory come to people who do not quit.

11. Build a mindset

When faced with tough situations, brainstorm. Think of solutions, ideas, alternatives, and possibilities for resolving the situation instead of giving up. There are various ways to work out a solution strategy by keeping your mind more open, flexible, and fearless. You may require a change in the approach or a slight strategy change. Recognize various ways to deal with a challenging or overwhelming situation.

### 12. Develop a sense of humor

This is a simple, easy, and enjoyable hack for people to develop mental toughness, yet a good number of people fail to see its virtues. When you experience challenges, humor can help you sail through the situation with ease. Look at the lighter side of things. This helps us overcome stress, disappointment, and anxiety connected to it. You gain a totally different perspective about challenges by viewing them using the lens of humor.

### 13. Build a positive or constructive view of your skills and abilities

An individual's sense of self-esteem, self-confidence, and self-image is mostly affected by perseverance. Keep reminding yourself about your strengths, achievements, skills, abilities, and beautiful moments. Make a list of tough situations you have tackled, and how you battled them. Draw inspiration from winning and decisive moments of the past.

### 14. Observe your self-talk

What is your mental talk sound like? If it isn't decisive, abundant, and prosperous, latch on to a different frequency. Our self-talk has the power to determine our chances of success. This self-talk can help us sail through challenging circumstances or dive into failure. Realign your self-talk for success by making it more positive, balanced, and constructive.

## Self-Discipline and Willpower

Self-discipline and willpower, alongside your significant level of certainty and inspiration, are critical in your endeavor to accomplish achievement. It advances self-improvement while likewise permitting you to make a tremendous, positive contrast in your life. Every one of them are useful in achieving your significant objectives as well as in satisfying straightforward, day by day errands.

So how would you develop both self-control and resolve?

Dispose of every single potential enticement

Remember that self-control is a constrained asset. All things considered, it's critical not to squander it. Each time you constrain yourself to disapprove of allurement without hiding it from you, you are likewise step by step exhausting your resolution. The issue is that it regularly requires some investment to renew it. On the off chance that conceivable, dispose of everything that you find enticing to abstain from losing your determination – expecting you to renew it regularly.

Make a strong arrangement

At the point when you notice your determination beginning to get exhausted, you can generally return to the arrangement you have created, just as the objective you have set, so you can alleviate the negative impacts of brought down self-control. While the facts confirm that even the individuals who have built up the most robust plans are still in danger of falling flat (since there's very assurance that you will be fruitful always), having it around will help keep you push ahead regardless of difficulties. This implies you'll keep attempting until you see all the means in your arrangement made into move.

Get enough sleep

Getting enough sleep is essential in allowing your brain to manage your energy more efficiently. It also plays a huge rule in ensuring that your prefrontal cortex works at its best. Depriving yourself of sleep, which usually happens when you just get less than six hours of sleep per night, can cause you to experience chronic stress, which tends to damage the way your brain and body utilize energy. Your prefrontal cortex suffers the blow the most, causing some parts of your brain, especially those that form cravings and stress response to lose control.

Improve the flexibility of your mind

Having a more resilient and flexible mind is crucial in boosting willpower. You can improve your mind's flexibility and resiliency by embracing changes and accepting challenges. With this improvement, it will be easier for your brain to form constructive responses to stressful circumstances. Your goal should be to direct your mind to what you want to achieve especially for the long term, instead of letting past failures and setbacks control you.

Make the most out of your imagination

Using your imagination is one of the most powerful techniques in boosting your discipline and willpower. Note that your body has the tendency to respond well to situations that you've imagined similar to the situations you actually experienced. For instance, imagining that you are currently in a peaceful beach allows your body to respond by relaxing. Imagining that you arrived at a meeting with your presentation unprepared may also cause your body to tense up. Your body's reaction to your imagination is actually useful in improving your willpower.

## How Mental Strength Improves Self-Discipline

Mental strength is one of the most important elements of self-discipline. Knowing how it contributes to self-discipline will help you to see why you need to be constantly working to enhance it.

When you are mentally strong, it allows you to conquer self-doubt so that it is not able to interfere with your level of discipline or cause you to procrastinate out of fear.

Motivation comes from your mental strength. When you are not mentally strong, you will find that it is much easier to lose your motivation before you even have a chance to take full advantage of it.

You can easily tune out comments and advice that are simply not going to help you. This is critical for self-discipline since it is all about efficiency and removing unnecessary baggage.

When you are mentally strong, you are able to face your fears. Fears are one of the biggest reasons that people are not able to develop a strong sense of self-discipline.

You can more easily rebound from failure with mental strength. When you quickly come back from failure, it's more difficult to disrupt your ability to be disciplined.

Learn from your mistakes. Remember that learning and accountability are paramount when working to enhance your discipline level.

# CHAPTER 6

# Practical Methods to Stop Procrastinating and Become more Productive

## 18 Practices to Stop Procrastination

1. Fill your calendar

Setting a schedule and using to-do lists are very helpful in keeping you organized, and ensuring you use your time efficiently. Schedules and to-do lists can take several different forms and depend on what you find most useful. You may need to dabble with several formats to find what works best for you. You may work better with lists or advanced project management software. Your schedule will be the goals, steps and smaller tasks that you need to complete on the way to this deadline, combined with a timeline.

2. Have a smart to do list

To-do lists tend to be more informal, but they can be put together more quickly. Also, the tasks listed in them do not need to be in a specific order. To-do lists can be particularly helpful in making you feel calmer and more control in anticipation of a day that is still a bit uncertain, but that you know will be busy.

3. Arrange your day into time chunks

When the feeling of a task being overwhelming is making you more likely to procrastinate, it can be extremely helpful to break the task down into "micro-tasks." These are the smaller tasks or steps that you need to take to complete a larger task.

4. Create a daily routine

Proper goal setting is one of the most important things you can do to help break your habit of procrastination. Good goal setting consists of the setting of achievable goals. Setting non-achievable goals is pointless and will just cause frustration and more procrastination. Setting goals correctly is a crucial step in the war against procrastination for three reasons:

1. When you achieve one of your goals, you gain a feeling of confidence. Better confidence in your abilities will make you less likely to put things off in fear of failure.

2. Goal setting will help you better organize your time and improve your prioritization skills. When you set clear goals, you will feel and be more organized. You will be better able to prioritize.

3. Goals help you organize your schedule. A properly set goal has a timeline and a way to measure success. You can then divide the target into daily pieces. If you want to lose thirty pounds in thirty days, you know that you need to lose one pound every day to hit your goal.

The more feelings of accomplishment you can put between you and a goal, the more likely you are to achieve it.

5.  Shorten your daily to do list

This is an advanced strategy, but it is one that has a lot of evidence behind it as a meaningful practice for avoiding procrastination. To approach this, we need to revisit why we procrastinate in the first place. There is at least one simple reason for procrastination: we do not want to do what needs to be done. Psychologists describe this as being part of emotion regulation. We seek what is called short-term mood repair and turn our attention away from the sources of our negative emotions. We avoid things that cause us stress, and this avoidance is manifested as procrastination. To work with negative feelings more comprehensively, we need to learn techniques that help us manage these moods and emotions in relation to those things that we cannot avoid, such as jobs and projects that require our attention. Mindfulness training and practices work well for this problem.

To properly manage negative emotions, we need a method that is effective for regulating feelings more generally. Mindfulness offers a comprehensive tool for managing emotions. It works to create present-moment awareness, which is precisely the thing we need to avoid procrastinating.

6.  Focus On one task at time

When a person in a workplace has a certain job to do, they might feel encouraged to get on that task and act as quickly as possible. However, not all people in the workplace feel the same way. Some people have their own individual reasons why they might want to do a particular chore and others might simply feel a lack of a desire to do it. All of these people are different because they are all being impacted by the concept of motivation in various ways. Some people might feel motivated to get to work, but their sources of motivation will come from different things. Some might be motivated by the potential to make money or to get a promotion. Others might be motivated to work with the fear that they might lose their jobs if they fail to work hard enough. Many people in the same environment might feel a distinct lack of motivation. These include people who feel they are incapable or that the task has no purpose. Others might just feel a sense of malaise or discontent.

Competition might be used as a source of motivation. While many people are motivated to help others and to be friendly, others could be motivated by focusing on their own achievements and treat a situation as a race between themselves and other people.

Whatever the case may be, it is vital to understand how motivation works and what makes it an effective tool in the workplace. It is an intriguing and extensive science in its own right, but it can be easily understood when the many aspects of the concept are reviewed.

7.   Schedule a weekly review

Most to-do lists are too long. They contain too many tasks. Consequently, many tasks are left unaddressed and remain unfinished at the end of the day. They must be carried forward to the following day or rescheduled for a future date. An unfinished to-do list has a demoralizing effect on us. It saps our motivation and injures our egos. And the more unfinished tasks that appear on our lists at the end of the day, the greater their impact. This problem increases the likelihood that we'll procrastinate. Faced with a long list of tasks and projects at the end of the day, we start to feel overwhelmed, buried under a mountain of unfinished work. Our stress levels rise, and it becomes difficult to make good decisions with regard to how to allocate our time best.

8. Evaluate your quarterly goals

Some tasks have massive impact. They move the needle in terms of our marriages, careers, income, and other aspects of our lives. Other tasks seem important, but actually have little impact on us. They have minimal lasting effect. When our priorities are vague, or we've prioritized tasks improperly, we end up spending our limited time on the wrong things. The small, inconsequential tasks capture our attention while the larger, more important - and often more difficult - tasks get placed on the back burner. This happens by way of procrastination. We delay taking action on big items by focusing on smaller, easier ones. We procrastinate on the big stuff by focusing our attention on the small stuff. We feel like we're getting a lot done, but our important work goes unaddressed. The solution is to reprioritize the items on your to-do list. Get clear on which tasks are crucial, which are not, and why. Distinguish those that move the needle from those that don't.

9. Take small steps

Think about how many things you have been postponing lately, and individually assess what the real reason for not doing the tasks is. Is it fear, laziness, or something else? Now, consider all the benefits you could gain if you started doing everything that you need to do, today. Make a mental list of all the pros. That should make you feel differently about procrastinating, and make you consider, at least in the back of your mind, doing all the things you need to do quickly instead of delaying them.

### 10. Visualization techniques

On the surface level, changing your thoughts might seem simple. After all, you think thousands of thoughts every single day, how hard can it really be for you to change what you are thinking? I will bet right now you can change your thought from this guidebook to something else, like the color of the wall in front of you, and then change it back to this guidebook all within a matter of a few seconds. Easy, right? Of course, it is.

It is always easy to change your thoughts when you are thinking about changing them. Remember, however, habit loops happen automatically and often without your conscious awareness, and many of your thoughts are a part of an automatic habit loop. For that reason, it can be a lot more challenging than you might think. In order to truly change your thoughts, you are going to have to start by first learning how to become aware of your thoughts and recognize what is going on in your mind. You need to not only recognize these thoughts retroactively but also recognize them at the moment as they are happening. This way, you identify the exact window of opportunity to change your thoughts, which will lead you to the opportunity to change away from thoughts that are triggering your procrastination behaviors.

Once you have identified your problematic thoughts, you can start brainstorming healthier thoughts for you to follow. Then, you can begin learning how to hold onto that thought for 17 seconds, then for 68 seconds. Lastly, you can learn how to apply this technique to multiple areas of your life because let us be honest; you can probably use the added boost! Procrastinating tends to touch down in all areas of life and can draw to sentiments of low self-esteem and low self-confidence, so leveraging this elsewhere in life will help you reverse your procrastinating behaviors and the unwanted symptoms you have gained from those behaviors.

11. Get rid of distractions

Regardless of whether its failure or fear, overwhelming feelings, convincing yourself that you are too busy to finish something, or avoidance, you can improve your capacity to be productive by killing your procrastination triggers.

Are You A Perfectionist? Usually, procrastination tendencies form because we have outgrown our goals. We are constantly changing and as we do, our wants and desires in life change as well. You need to look over your goals and then ask yourself whether they still apply.

## CHAPTER 7

# Learning to say Yes and No

Saying no is another part of the anti-procrastination process that will be difficult to implement. Again, not because it's hard to do, but because it requires a deep level of commitment that most people don't have when it comes to their personal goals.

What does this have to do with procrastination? Well, there are three reasons why this step is an important part of the process.

First, by now you know that the feeling of overwhelm is often the biggest cause of procrastination. When you feel like you have too much to do daily, it's easy to push off the difficult stuff because you don't have the physical or mental bandwidth to do them well.

Second, it's also easy to fall into the trap of agreeing to the requests for your time from other people simply because you don't want to disappoint anyone. We all want to be liked, so we'll agree to something—even when we know it's something, we don't have time to do.

Finally, it's easy to "tinker" on projects that sound fun but aren't part of your five core projects. This is a dangerous practice, because whenever you say yes to something new, you're basically saying no to the projects that you've already identified as being important.

While you picked 5 core projects, you also had to say no to the other 20. The problem here is that they are 20 items in which you have some personal interest. Unfortunately, on some level, they can be the biggest distraction of them all because you'll often feel the occasional urge (possibly induced by a bit of guilt) to focus on these activities.

Of course, a portion of these thoughts are unrealistic—they are container list thoughts that sound great, yet I'm as of now uncertain of how they'll fit into my timetable. Then again, there are a couple of thoughts that I couldn't imagine anything better than to do now, however I perceive that time invested on them is energy detracted from the five tasks that are imperative to me.

Thus, at this point you know it's essential to disapprove of whatever contentions with the center tasks throughout your life.

The inquiry is: "How would I say no without ticking individuals off or falling into difficulty at work?"

**All things considered; you can do this by building five practices into your everyday practice.**

Practice #1: Say No as Early and Politely as could be expected under the circumstances

Be straightforward with individuals about their solicitations. In the event that you realize you can't finish on an undertaking, at that point be firm and disclose to them immediately.

Trustworthiness truly is the best approach here. Essentially tell the individual that you have a couple of need extends that require your complete consideration and you can't manage the cost of the interruption. Normally, a great many people will comprehend the need to concentrate on the need undertakings.

Attempt to finish strong. In the event that you can't enable the individual, to suggest somebody who can. On the off chance that you are aware of a supportive asset, offer that as another option. What's more, in the event that you feel that you may allow the solicitation soon, at that point request that the individual follow up on a particular date.

Saying no doesn't make you a narrow minded individual. It makes you somebody who obviously comprehends what's significant. By having clear objectives, you don't permit the requests of others to occupy you from finishing significant tasks.

Practice #2: Identify the Mandatory Tasks

We as a whole have commitments that aren't generally fun yet at the same time should be finished on the grounds that they're an essential piece of being a typical, composed grown-up. As such, in the event that you disapprove of each solicitation for your time, you most likely won't get much of anywhere throughout everyday life.

We as a whole have things that must be done, so you may as a well acknowledge that you need to get things done, regardless of the amount you don't care for them.

My lone counsel is to relate each assignment to one of the five center activities that you've recently recognized.

Practice #3: Compare Each Request to Your Current Projects

As the German military planner Helmuth von Moltke once stated, "No fight plan endures contact with the foe."

The exercise that I take from this statement is while it's anything but difficult to focus on just five activities intellectually, it's an entire other test to continue through to the end whenever you find new chances or get demands for your time from the individuals throughout your life.

That is the reason I enthusiastically suggest taking a couple of moments at whatever point there's a solicitation for your opportunity to look at it against your present needs and ventures.

You've just distinguished what's critical to you, so when you get a solicitation to accomplish something, contrast it with your ideal results. In the event that they don't coordinate, at that point have the boldness to disapprove of the requester.

Here's a straightforward three-section procedure to rapidly assess any solicitation for your time:

1.      Compare the new chance to your present rundown of five tasks. Is there a current venture that is not as significant as the upgraded one? Assuming this is the case, ask yourself what the most direct outcome imaginable would be in the event that you expelled it from your life or put it on pause.

2.      Figure out the motivation behind why you may be keen on supplanting one of your current undertakings. Is it since you've hit a difficult deterrent? It is safe to say that you are concerned that you'll commit an error. Have you been disappointed at the absence of obvious outcomes? It is safe to say that you are exhausted with it.

These are imperative inquiries to pose in light of the fact that occasionally our craving to begin something new originates from a dread of standing up to a significant snag. It's alright to kill existing objectives and tasks—simply ensure you're doing it for the correct reasons.

3.      If you can't supplant an old task however you despite everything need to chip away at the upgraded one, at that point figure what can be wiped out from your life. Maybe you may be happy to diminish your TV

time by an hour or two consistently, or possibly you can diminish the time spent on your preferred side interest.

The one thing to remember is that when you include new activities, that additional opportunity needs to arrive from some place. Along these lines, on the off chance that you need to include another center, you'll have to forfeit time that is committed to something different.

Your life will consistently be loaded up with demands for your time. This is particularly obvious as you manufacture your vocation and your time turns out to be progressively looked for after. That is the point at which you have to recognize what's genuinely essential to you and so forth. On the off chance that you neglect to make firm limits throughout your life, at that point your spare time will be chipped away by a steady reiteration of solicitations.

Practice #4: Talk to Your Boss about Your Top Projects

While it sounds decent on paper to concentrate just on ventures identified with your objectives, at times you have to confront the circumstance and work on undertakings that you probably won't appreciate.

Clearly, you can't disapprove of your chief and hope to remain productively utilized for long. Be that as it may, in the event that you feel overpowered at your particular employment since you have many errands, you may need to have a real to life discussion to diminish a portion of your activity pressures. Here are four techniques for conversing with your supervisor to ensure you're dealing with the essential tasks that are genuinely significant for the business for which you work:

1.      Do your schoolwork early. Recognize the a few normal errands that give the greatest effect on the organization's primary concern. This ought to be the exercises that you're getting paid to finish. Next, distinguish the customary assignments that impede these center exercises. In a perfect world, this ought to be errands that could be designated or essentially wiped out from your day.

2.      Schedule a period with your chief and quickly notice the motivation behind why you need to meet. This will offer her the chance to get ready for the gathering and give accommodating input. This notification ahead of time is significant on the grounds that you don't need your supervisor to feel like you're tossing something at her that requires a quick choice.

3.      Start the discussion by conceding that you've been battling to stay aware of your work ventures. Discussion about the a few high-influence undertakings that you've recognized early as being significant. Inquire as to whether she concurs that these are your needs. In the event that not, at that point ask her what she would consider to be significant about your activity. Continue posing inquiries and examining until you both can go to a concurrence on what you should concentrate on day by day.

4.      Talk about how certain ventures and arbitrary assignments impede your capacity to concentrate on these basic undertakings. Normally the greatest guilty parties are gatherings, email, and irregular

disturbances. Certainly, they may regularly appear to be pressing, however they frequently can transform into time-sucking errands that cause you to dawdle on the exercises that are really significant.

The way in to the adequacy of this progression is to not whine about being exhausted yet to give arrangements on the best way to fix this issue. These recommendations can incorporate skipping gatherings that aren't straightforwardly identified with your center a few errands; killing the undertakings that don't legitimately line up with your needs; appointing certain obligations that don't line up with your center assignments to colleagues or subordinates; mentioning an impermanent specialist or new worker to alleviate the burden; and carrying out specific responsibilities on a less successive premise (e.g., week after week rather than day by day or month to month rather than week by week).

Without a doubt, setting off to your chief and conceding that you can't do everything may appear to be a startling discussion. In any case, what you're doing is attempting to realign your time so you can concentrate on the exercises that create the greatest benefit for the organization. On the off chance that you can show that dispensing with the irrelevant prompts an expansion in profitability, the discussion ought to be a simple choice with regards to getting what you need.

Practice #5: Ask Yourself, "What Will My Obituary Say?"

It's anything but difficult to state no in the event that you continually consider the significant things throughout your life. One approach to do this is to envision what will be written in your tribute.

Think about the words in your brain at the present time. Okay lean toward a depiction that discussions about positive things, similar to how you were a caring guardian, extraordinary mate, world explorer, dynamic individual from your strict network, and somebody who adored life? Or on the other hand would you pick a tribute that depicts how you said yes to each extend, worked late around evening time, and consistently picked your vocation over your own objectives?

Ideally, you picked the principal choice—I realize that is the portrayal that I would like.

At the point when you adjust yourself to your objectives and reliably disapprove of whatever doesn't coordinate your present center, you'll save time to concentrate on the exercises that merit finding out about when you arrive at an amazing finish.

CHAPTER 8

# The Daily Habits You Need to Embrace to Strengthen Your Mind and Harden your Determination

As we have said, procrastination can be both avoided and cured. One of the best ways to do that is to create good habits. In order to ultimately overcome procrastination, you have to nurture positive habits instead of just implementing short-term actions. Now, you will discover 3 positive habits that you should cultivate, as well as how to attack the root cause of your procrastination.

## The 3 Habits that You Should Nurture

Habit 1: Spend about 5 minutes planning your week.

Sunday night may be a good time to do this, though some people prefer to do this on Friday before the weekend. The actual day doesn't matter, as long as you set aside 5 minutes to do this. Try doing this on different days if you're not sure what suits you.

You should plan your week both professionally and personally, but also set aside time for yourself to simply do what you like.

Your personal tasks may include:

- The weekly grocery shopping and planning your meals.

- Booking and going to any medical appointments.

- Maintaining your home and addressing any technical household problems.

- Hobbies and leisure activities, including sports or outings with friends.

When considering your professional tasks:

- Organize your tasks in order of priority, from more to less urgent.

- Prioritize urgent tasks that you have to finish that week.

- Keep track of tasks that are in progress, but do not depend on you.

- Set yourself goals for that week and check them.

By the end of the week, you will see that you have achieved more than you think.

Habit 2: Eliminate distractions.

If you want to finish a specific task, do not be distracted by other stimuli. Below is an example of how you can apply this method to a real scenario.

Imagine that you have several tasks to do:

1.     Finish writing a document.

2.     Prepare for a new project or assignment.

3.     Submit an application.

You need to focus on these tasks and finish them all in less than 4 hours.

To help do this, you should:

• Put your phone out of sight, so you aren't tempted to keep checking it.

• Close all irrelevant programs and tabs on your computer.

• Avoid surfing the Internet, except if specifically required for a task.

• Avoid checking any social media.

Finally, allocate time to each task and keep to your deadlines:

1st hour: Finish writing the document.

Before moving onto the next task, reward yourself by making tea or having a treat.

2nd hour: Draft your plan and note important points for the new project.

When you finish, disconnect for 10 minutes by doing another task that you like more.

3rd Hour: Complete the application and submit it.

With your last half hour, you can answer any unread emails or messages.

Habit 3: Reward yourself for your efforts but be flexible.

If you execute your tasks at a good pace, reward yourself afterwards. Take a short break before starting the next task—you can have a tea or coffee or make a short phone call to a friend.

You can also reward yourself at the end of the day and again at the end of the week. You should decide what rewards are the best incentives to complete your tasks, as well as what your "punishment" is if you do not meet your daily or weekly goals.

Some examples are:

Incentives: Meet friends, go to the movies, buy something, go jogging.

Penalties: Ban yourself from using your phone or laptop for a short period of time, go jogging.

Depending on the person, jogging can be an incentive or punishment!

It is important to be flexible with ourselves, as we are not as motivated every day. Find the balance between the demands of your workload and what you can reasonably achieve.

## Attacking the Root of the Problem

The best way to attack procrastination at the root is to design your tasks in a way that doesn't even leave a margin for it. Here are some ideas.

Idea 1: Choose your tasks well

If you systematically procrastinate in your studies or in your job, it is because you are not getting into the flow. And if you don't get into the flow—we're sorry to tell you, but maybe you're in the wrong subject or industry.

The flow has nothing to do with passion; it does not mean going through a whole day feeling uninterrupted. Instead, it is about selecting tasks that allow you to maintain a state of optimal concentration. If you are required by your studies or job to do tasks that "violate your will regularly", you are extremely likely to end up burned out.

Sure, you may say: "But I'm not going to change my degree or job to get into the flow. Could you give me more realistic advice?"

Of course, you don't have to put yourself in the radical mode of give-up-my-work-and-I-go-with-my-backpack. But the first step is to realize that the problem is not in you, but in the task and how it makes you feel.

Maybe this horrible task that you always procrastinate only gives you a very small benefit in your job or studies. Consider whether you can reduce the extent of the task somehow, eliminate it by delegating to someone else, or get the same task done in a different way.

Idea 2: Eliminate other "habitual suspects": perfectionism, burning out, etc.

It is worth considering that procrastination might be your friend and is here to help you. You may find that the underlying problem has nothing to do with motivation.

• Perhaps what it needs is to save you from your perfectionism, from your own belief that you are not enough, and to get you away from the risk of completing the task.

• Maybe it wants you to rest.

• Maybe it is here because you haven't spent enough time thinking about a good idea for your project, and now you're bored like a monkey.

In that case, the solution is not your willpower. The solutions are, in this order: abandon perfectionism, rest more and come up with new ideas.

Sometimes procrastination is your body telling you that you need to get away a little and think more about what you're doing. Don't stay in a loop in front of the computer, browsing Facebook non-stop and feeling guilty. Think. And then, act differently than how you have been so far.

Idea 3: Use deadlines

"Keep working and send it to me when it's ready." Alert, alert! If you have a tendency to procrastinate, then don't accept this from your professor or manager. Tell yourself this: "No, I'd rather set a deadline so I can organize myself better."

Pick a deadline and stick to it. Publicly commit to the person who needs you to complete the task: "I will have it finished for you on that day without fail."

Idea 4: Plan far in advance

On your calendar, find the dates for an important project and change them to one or two weeks earlier. Note the minimum time you'd need to do a good job, then when the time comes, start with enthusiasm.

But what if an unforeseen circumstance arises?

Remember, focusing on any project creates some chaos in the rest of our lives. It's inevitable and it's positive. It is not a question of maintaining balance, but of unbalancing in different directions.

So, what do you do if an unforeseen circumstance arises? In 99% of cases, you will have the capacity to figure out how to reorganize your task. In the remaining 1%, the chances are that the seriousness of the unexpected does not really impact your final outcome.

## The 5-Minute Solution

We will now introduce the key solution to this guidebook: The 5-minute solution.

It is essential that you implement the tips from this 5-minute solution, as together they serve as the fundamental idea for overcoming procrastination.

This strategy is fairly straightforward, so don't be surprised if you expected a more complicated description. Others have varied this little strategy to 2 minutes or 10 minutes. However, in this guidebook, we will concentrate on habits you can create in 5 minutes

Most of the things that you procrastinate are, in fact, hard to do because you have the talent and skills to complete them. You simply avoid doing the tasks for other reasons. The 5-minute solution tackles procrastination by making it easier to start each task.

There are three parts to the 5-minute solution.

Part 1: Whatever the task is, spend 5 minutes on it

What has proven most effective in overcoming procrastination is based on what is called the 5-minute solution.

So, instead of saying that you have to spend the whole morning working on a project or writing material for a marketing campaign, just start with 5 minutes.

If it's a phone call, pick up the phone and make the call. If you need to submit an article, write as much as you can in 5 minutes. Maybe your work will be brilliant or maybe it won't, but it doesn't matter; the fundamental thing is that you will have broken the cycle and shown that you can face stress.

That eliminates the main blow that procrastination throws at you. It is the psychological anxiety that makes you look at a task and only see how hard it will be.

Knowing that you're only going to be 5 minutes reduces that anxiety to a large extent because it's such a small amount of time.

Part 2: Do a countdown of 5

When the time has come to do something, your instincts ignite. You know you have to do it, but you feel doubt. That is the moment when you have to do a countdown of 5 before you get going. This can be 5 seconds or 5 minutes, etc. If within 5 minutes you don't start doing what you need to, your brain will abandon the idea and you will convince yourself to leave it for another time.

Part 3: Do tasks for 25 minutes and rest 5 minutes

The third part of the 5-minute solution is to improve productivity is based on doing a task across 10, 15 and 25 minutes, then resting for 5 minutes.

As an example, imagine that you have to prepare a business email that will take 25 minutes in total. You take between 10 and 15 minutes to write an email and then another 10 minutes to send it to a mailing list. Then you can take about 5 minutes of rest to talk with a friend on social media, watch the news, have a coffee or a tea, etc. Every 25 minutes, you should set small goals to reach. Each goal must include an objective with a 5-minute break.

We have discovered that this is the best mentality to apply, because if we set aside 5 minutes knowing that the task will really 50, then the psychological anxiety of the task is not reduced.

The most significant piece of another propensity is to begin—the first run through, yet without fail. It's not about execution, yet reliably making a move. From numerous points of view, beginning is a higher priority than succeeding. This is particularly obvious to start with on the grounds that there will be a ton of time to improve your presentation later on.

The brief arrangement isn't about the outcomes you need to accomplish, however the procedure of really carrying out the responsibility. This works best for individuals who accept that the framework is a higher priority than the objective. The attention is on acting and letting things stream from it.

We can't ensure that the brief arrangement will work for you, however we can promise you that it won't work in the event that you don't attempt.

## CHAPTER 9

# Looking to Success

S uccess may be happiness, work security, making a lot of money or achieving a target. Everybody's idea of accomplishment may be unique. However, a way to get success is to be productive.

What exactly does beneficial mean?

Being productive is creating, producing richly, bringing about a result. Being productive and achieving isn't something that happens overnight.

You need to buckle down, train yourself have willpower and have inspiration. Being productive also means overseeing your time, having propensity, following a schedule, focusing, being organized, and avoiding interferences.

If you carry on with your life being apathetic it can genuinely be hard. You probably won't have a ton of money or accomplishment. If you carry on with your life buckling down it can make life easier. You will be ready to get the more significant part of the things that you need. They say, everything is possible with a little bit of conviction. The habits I shall be a list that will act like a guide to a complete transformation in your lifestyle. Success is a gradual process and it requires patience as much as it requires determination but adopting these qualities and turning them into routines will help you get where you want to. Here is a little handbook with a few simple steps, one you embed these into your system, success is the next logical step.

## Handbook to Success

Step 1: Staying Focused

Selective focus is kind, smart focus is better. You need to remember at all times that if you're giving the job at hand your all, it will never rise to your expectation. Even if the job is small, give it all your attention and give it all your time. The operative word here is 'prioritize.' This is why I talk about smart focus. Analyze what needs your immediate attention and then dedicate all your attention to it. Environment plays a vital work in helping you focus. If you feel like you can't work at home, pull an all-nighter at your office. If it's the festive season, make sure you make arrangements in advance to find yourself a quite isolated spot that leaves you alone with your work. Once you've prioritized and settled to work don't stray. It's a good habit to take small breaks, in fact it's healthy. But the job has to be done no matter what, and getting distracted mid-way and worst of all don't procrastinate. Remember the old adage, better now than never? Implement it. Staying focused also allows you to take up one small goal at a time. This allows you to simply work towards one minor attainable achievement rather than worry about the bigger picture. Let this achievement breed confidence that carry you through other short-term goals and finally to the ultimate goal.

## Step 2: Work on Your Strengths

Specialize don't generalize. Don't be jack of all, master of none. Let this be the motto of your life. This habit in fact is an extension of the first point. Working on your strengths implies that you concentrate all your focus in the direction of already developed skills. Don't let yourself get disenchanted by talents once achievement becomes a habit. It is essential to develop new skills and become resourceful continuously but it is more important always to keep your knife sharpened and polish. Don't pick up new skill sets and abandon old ones; those are the only ones you can fall back on. If you are working as a business analyst, it is good to broaden your horizon and learn about something new, like theatre for example. But don't lose sight of your primary occupation. This is the breadwinner of your skill family.

## Step 3: Thrift Is a Virtue

According to Confucius goes thus, "he who will not economize will have to agonize." Make frugality a habit. Spend wisely live economically. Most wealthy men live extremely humble lives. If you are in your thirties, start saving for retirement. Especially if you have a family to support. Don't let lifestyle statements and advertising media compel you into spending carelessly. When you will need money for investment, you will find yourself only with Armani suits. Look at it as a long-term investment. Working on your financing now will take you a long way. Reserve cash always helps you save yourself some worry when really in need. Why get yourself to such a point, think about how big you want to get and save for your own growth.

Step 4: Handpick Your Team

The prospect of working with better qualified people may seem like a daunting task, but don't shy away from it. Working with less qualified people works only to boost your ego, and any successful business man will tell you that that is the first thing you should get rid of. Instead always looks forward to learning more. Working with more successful people might make you feel small and insignificant but it will teach you a lot. Anyone can be the big fish in his small lake, but shinning out in a well-qualified, hardworking team is difficult and challenging. Let this challenge motivate you to be a better worker. Don't let emotions blur your judgements with colleagues, emotional support only has so much use in business. Work towards efficiency and productivity and keep this in mind while choosing your team. The people you work with will not only affect the overall productivity of the team; they will affect your own attitude towards the work. A lackadaisical team can leave you with a very low self-esteem and the burden of a job done. Let yourself be surrounded by people who inspire you.

## Step 5: Retrospect

Chose any time of your convenience for this. Back from work, before dinner, first thing in the morning, or right before sleep. Anything will do as long as you feel you can give your hundred percent to the job. If you feel saturated after returning home, don't use that time to do a recap of your entire day. You need to be able to judge the events of the day objectively. This is possible only if you are feeling calm and fresh. Go through the notes you made all day long, the correspondence on your mail and the conversations you had on your phone. Did you make an outstanding deal today? If so, are you planning to follow it up with something soon? What will that be? Do you feel dissatisfied with something you gave in today? Tomorrow is the latest you can make the change; delays are unprofessional think it through before you reach for work and have a Plan of Action.

## Step 6: Strategy for the Day

While you sit and go over the events of the day, it usually makes sense to work proactively towards changing the things that left you with a bitter taste. Note down a strategy for the same. Refer your notes/calendars/reminders and decide what needs to be done tomorrow. Don't worry too much about the ultimate goal, but keep it in mind. Go one day at a time.

At the same time have long term goals, five-year plans and three-year plans are a great way of ensuring organized expansion. That way you never sway off track even while you concentrate on immediate goals. A time chart is your best friend and will help you keep a track of your activities, which means you'll end up saving a lot of your invaluable time.

A POA is a process in itself. The list will keep building itself as you get closer to your office. This is why it makes sense to have everything written down in the form of a list. If it is a long list, you know what you are signing up for, you are going to be ready by the time you reach.

## Step 7: Make Persistence A Habit

When you are faced with obstacles, persevere. This diligent push will see you through all the ups and downs of a job. Giving up is not an option, that is not how success is achieved. Persistence is a result of concentrating all your strengths, it comes with the right focus. Only if a job has your complete attention, can you solve the problems that try to deter you from your goal. If you have your feet in more than one boat, you can't fight the tide. Push towards success with all your strength, and if something tries to push you back, let inertia be your guide. Push back with an equal and opposite force.

## Step 8: Work on Your Health

Work is important but not at the cost of your health. An unhealthy body also fails at being productive. Illness brings discomfort and with that, distraction. If you have the foresight to think about your career on a long-term basis, take care of your health from right now. Go for daily check-ups, stay away from painkillers and unnecessary drugs. Don't rely on them for giving you the strength to work; it will only do you bad in the long run. A rest for a day is better than an early retirement.

Successful men cultivate some or the other healthy habit, jog for an hour, do yoga. Stay fit. Only a healthy horse wins the race. Small habits can also go a long way, take the stairs, cut down on the coffee or switch to decaf. Eat your meals at fixed timings and sleep early.

Step 9: Calculated Risks

Risk is as important as hard work to success and even more indispensable. But be smart while dealing with them. Don't be over-achieving, calculate the pros and cons of your risk and then take the proverbial dive.

Make it a habit to research the possibilities of your step. Read about it, talk to friends and experts. Responsible risk taking has to be cultivated, it doesn't come naturally. And because it is meticulous, you will find yourself slacking off and jumping into something big with dangerous abandon. A business cannot rely on chances. It needs to be based on the strong foundations of analyzed steps and responsible risks.

Step 10: Pause. Take A Break. Relax

Give yourself a break once in a while. You deserve it. You might be working on a very tight schedule, on the most important project of the year. Don't say you don't have time for a break. Resting is not falling back on your work. It helps you pace yourself and prepare for the job to do. Your brain cannot keep working consistently without any breaks.

Of course, this doesn't mean that your office hours should be made up entirely of breaks. Take off a few minutes from your lunch time to calm yourself, have the green tea you substituted your smoke with, and log out. A power nap is also very good idea sometimes; many offices even offer their employees with bunkers for the same.

Several professions even have compulsory rest hours, like a pilot's profession. This is because a minimal amount of rest is necessary for the mind to display concentration and vigilance.

The listed habits are just some of the good habits you could adopt. They are a result of my observations of successful people. You may cultivate other habits as they complement your work or as they suit your fancy. Let your instinct and judgement help you through this process. Keep your profession and the ultimate goal always in mind and make your list. Remember, always have a POA. This is a part of your long term POA.

CHAPTER 10

# Caring for Oneself with Self-Hypnosis

## Guide on Self-Hypnosis

Give in to my voice and allow me to carry you to a mindful space. Lie down and relax. Or sit down if you feel more comfortable doing so but this exercise is best when you are laying down. Make sure that you are in a room with a closed door and open windows. Feel the fresh breeze touch your skin softly as you sit there. Take a moment to think about why you are doing this. Focus on a single thought to make yourself aware of your reason for entering this state of mind. Close your eyes once you have it.

Visualize your idea in your mind, give it a shape and size. I will give you a moment to do this. Become aware of your surroundings while you're doing this. Start by focusing on the fibers of your duvet. Is it soft? Feel the duvet on your skin and listen to my voice as you take a deep breath and hold it for a second. Now release your breath slowly through your mouth.

Listen to the sound of the breeze. I know you can feel it but now I want you to listen to it. Listen to the faint whistle it makes as it passes through the window. Be aware of the fact that it's making a sound. Now I want you to rewind for a moment, back to your worrisome idea. The idea you

90

have chosen to bring to the surface, something you have chosen to avoid for some time now. You are going to avoid it a little longer. Follow my instructions closely as you take your idea that now has a shape and wrap it in a fancy box. Close the box and feel your left hand place the imaginary box beside you. Remember that you have visualized an idea, a thought. It doesn't have a physical form.

Now I want you to focus deeper on my voice. Yes, you can do it. Return your left hand to your side and caress your duvet. Feel the intricate fibers between your fingers. Continue doing this while you inhale deeply and hold. One, two, and release. Remember to release your breath slowly because there is no rush. Now I want you to take your right hand and place it on your stomach and run your fingertips gently up and down your skin. Become aware of the connection between your fingertips and the skin on your stomach. You feel a light friction.

Open your mind to my suggestion and change your finger strokes from up and down, to circles. Focus on the friction between your fingers and skin. This sensation is what release feels like. The friction is your body's tension being drawn out by your fingertip movement. The friction is moving into your right hand and going up your arm. It travels through your chest area and into your left arm from there. Follow the friction as it travels down your left arm and into the duvet fibers you are holding with your fingertips. Keep inhaling gently, holding it each time for a moment before release. All your tension is leaving your body. Focus your awareness on the tension exiting through every breath you take, through every stroke of your fingers running over your skin.

You are listening to my voice on an even deeper level now. You can hear it inside your mind, telling you what to do. I want you to start moving your right hand and keep your left hand beside your body, holding the duvet. Don't disconnect yourself from this outlet. You will remove the outflow of your tension. Don't stop breathing gently while you move your right hand up and down your body to every place you can reach. Keep circling your fingertips and following the tension out of your left arm.

Now I need you to concentrate. I want you to start wiggling your toes gently. Focus on the movement and the way you feel as you do this. This helps to send the tension up to your circling fingertips. You won't miss any tension this way. Move your awareness to your level of relaxation once you feel comfortable. Your entire body has sunk into a relaxed state as my voice stays with you every moment of the journey. Every word I utter brings you one step closer to your comfort. You feel safe in the guidance you are allowing.

Now I want you to become aware of your new surroundings. It's time to awaken your mind's eye. You need to continue breathing deep and consistent breaths, pausing for a moment between each inhale and exhale. Shift your attention to your left hand beside you. Can you feel the leaves under your fingertips? Move your left hand around and become aware of the leaves around you. Now take your right hand and do the same. Listen to my voice as I help you feel your body on the pile of soft leaves. My voice is even deeper in your mind now. Controlling your hands through gentle guidance. You feel so calm and safe.

I want you to start creating an image. Pay close attention to my calm and instructive voice as my words become your image. Use your imagination to create this picture while you lay there and breathe consistently. I want you to count to ten. Count quietly in your mind. Now open your beautiful inner eyes and see what you have created. You are looking at tall trees standing over you with rays of sunlight dancing between them. You can feel yourself growing an urge to explore this beautiful nature before you as you raise yourself to a seated position. You see the prettiest purple flowers under the trees. They are bountiful with the perfect balance of sun and shade from the trees. Feel yourself rise as you approach the flowers to smell them.

My voice keeps guiding you as you walk toward the flowers and kneel to pick one. You notice a small stairway leading downward behind the trees as you lift the fragrant flower to your nose and you feel a strong desire to follow the overgrown stairway. It looks like no one has been down here in awhile. Follow me down as I descend the staircase. You can see the stairway leads down to a wooden cabin as your foot touches the first step. The vegetation surrounding the cabin is beautiful and exotic, something from an unknown world. You feel the need to know more even though the cabin looks abandoned. You can smell all the amazing flowers as you descend step by step. Each step makes you relax a little more, each makes you feel safer.

You are enjoying the journey so much that you are falling behind. You will find my voice at the bottom of the stairway. You continue your descent, step by step. My voice gets louder as you catch up but you are also aware of the sounds around you. Birds are chirping in the trees and you are sure you can hear something in the bush. You still feel calm and safe because nothing can harm you here. You can hear water flowing over rocks in the distance. The flow of water is strong and seems to match your urge to get to the cabin. Take a moment to enjoy the sound. You don't need to rush to the cabin. It will come in good time.

You focus your attention back to my voice after a moment of reflection in this amazingly wild and untouched area. My voice is urging you to climb the three steps to the cabin door. You count the steps as you climb them. One, two, and three. The cabin looks more deserted now that you are closer. This doesn't persuade you to leave because you need to know what's inside. Before you do, take a deep breath in through your nose and hold. One, two, and slowly release the air from your mouth.

Let my voice guide you inside and focus on my every word. You feel more relaxed with each one. You place your hand on the door knob and feel the cold touch your skin. You feel yourself hesitate for a moment. Take a deep breath and hold. Release your Procrastination through your breath. Now you are free to turn the knob. You push the door gently as you turn it. It creaks ever so slightly as you open it. You see piles and piles of boxes from floor to ceiling inside. Please don't be afraid and step inside.

You can feel the air is thicker here than outside. The cabin has been abandoned for too long now and is filled with dust bunnies. You proceed forward with my guidance anyway. You know where you are; you know exactly who abandoned this place. This is your subconscious cabin and it's overflowing with things that need to be taken care of. You feel the urge to tackle the tasks in the boxes as you stand there. Now listen to me carefully because I am aware that you feel confident now. I am also aware that you realize your problem but you need to become aware that you can't do it all at once.

Feel yourself accepting the fact and start organizing your boxes. You can separate them into four different corners. Inhale deeply through your nose and hold. One, two, and three. Now exhale gently as you see how the boxes have piled up. You are more than capable of working through them in an orderly fashion. Make one corner an urgent corner, the other corner can be for less urgent tasks, the third corner is for tasks that can wait a little and the last corner can be for tasks you must decide if you wish to proceed. Can you see how organized it all looks now? See how much easier it will be to finish these tasks? Now it's time to go home.

Listen to my voice to guide you back as you remain aware of your feelings and the sounds around you. Leave the door unlocked when you go. This is your safe house and no one will find it. Retrace your steps back up the staircase and pay attention to the vegetation around it. It's been cut back. It remains stunning but the stairway is clear. Take one more sniff of the flowers under the trees before you lay down on the leaves. Now I want you to focus on your breathing. Deep breath in and hold. One, two, and release gently. Lay your arms beside you and feel your surroundings. Become aware of the duvet under your fingertips. Breathe in deep and hold. One, two, and release the air gently. Feel your body return to its physical form. The cool touch of the breeze passing over you as the sound of the breeze passes through the window. Now I want you to reach to your left and pick up the box you placed beside you. Open it and visualize the one idea you stored in the box. This will be your first task to complete.

Focus on my voice as you feel your physical presence resuming itself. Now open your eyes and repeat after me. I am aware of my new strength and ability. Say it another three times. Notice how refreshed you feel, physically, and emotionally. Feel your burning desire to finish your task so you may visit your cabin again to collect another. My voice seems further and further away as you are now awake and fully aware of your present surroundings

# CHAPTER 11

# Setting to Achieve the Objectives

Having clear set goals will help to mobilize your focus and effort towards meeting the desired objective which is overcoming procrastinating. Setting goals for yourself will build your confidence and also help you to increase your productivity.

First of all, you need to take time and think about what your goals are. These should be divided into long term and short-term goals. Your short-term goals should facilitate your long-term goals. Write them all down on a list and work out how much time you think it will take to achieve all of these. You have been active in goal setting and not just thinking of them passively in your mind. If you want to stay motivated towards your goals, you have to create some milestones. These will be your short-term goals. When you pass each milestone, you will know how much closer you are to your long-term goal. It will help you stay focused while tracking your progress.

Setting a goal will trigger your behavior. When you know what you want, your focus can be on working toward achieving this. Someone without a goal will just drift through their days being unproductive and aimless. Setting a goal will naturally direct your focus towards it. It will lead you in the direction that is right for you. While you achieve your short-term goals, you will realize that it is addictive. This will help to sustain momentum and help you stay focused in the long term. It will also help to build character. Your goals will help you identify the kind of person you are and what your priorities are. This is why you need to set goals, manage them and improve further.

## Goal Setting Myths

To make sure you don't set yourself up to fail, then you must know what myths you might believe about goal setting. You can have the very best of intentions if you've got the wrong idea about what goal setting is, then all the best intentions in the world will not help you become more productive. Let's look at the various myths about goal-setting you believe that could be setting you up to fall flat on your face.

1.Goal setting is pointless. What often inspires this thinking is the idea that you really cannot predict the future, and as such, you should not even bother setting goals. I get it. Really. However, there's a little something called "mental forecasting." Sometimes the weather person says it's going to be sunny all day, and then next thing you know, it's raining. Go figure. For the most part, you know you can trust the forecasts. This is the same thing we're talking about here.

Understandably, there will be speed bumps along the way of achieving your goals, but when you set your goals the right way, you make room for the unpredictable stuff. Kind of like carrying an umbrella just in case of a shower. Setting your goals, the right way will give you the tools you need to keep going, especially when things happen that make you want to quit or make you stressed out. This is just one more reason that the SMART method is not so smart.

3. I've set goals before. It didn't work. Never will. It's fascinating that some people think this way. It's like, you fell in love, but it didn't work out, and so there's no such thing as love, you say. There are several reasons why goal setting may not have worked for you. It could be a matter of the circumstances or the timing of things. Or, you could have chosen a goal setting method that just doesn't work for you. Or you set your goals the wrong way. None of this automatically means goal setting doesn't work for you. All you need is to learn from your previous attempts so that you do not repeat the same behaviors that lead to your failure.

4. Systems matter more than goals. The funny thing about this myth is that goals and systems are two peas in a pod. They're two sides of a coin. You can't have one without the other. When you set a goal, you must take action. This is where your system comes to play. When you have a system, no matter how effective it is, if you have no goals, then there's

nothing to tell you whether or not you're being productive or being busy. Systems are the tools with which you can reach your set goals.

5. Not reaching goals makes you a failure. No, it doesn't. You need to adjust your mindset. That the goal was not accomplished might have nothing to do with you. The problem may lie with the method and tools you used to try making that goal a reality. Perhaps your product or service hasn't achieved the goal you've set, because there was a problem with your product design, or with the marketing.

You would do well to look at failure in a different light. Think of them as temporary setbacks. A setback is just that. You can take some time to reevaluate where you're at, where you're going, and how you're getting there. You can readjust your deadline and keep on going. Focus on the fact that you've made it so far and learn from what went wrong so you can keep going further.

6. There's no need to write down your goals. You do. When your goals are only in your head, then they won't be very clear. You won't be able to take exact actions. You'll just keep winging it. Unless you have a lot of dumb luck, winging it is not the way to achieve your goals.

You need to write them down and keep them visible. This way, everything you do is about your goal. You can see it. You can take time to reflect on it and see how you're doing. You can use it to inspire you to do more and be better. Write down your goals. This will improve your focus and make distractions powerless. You will automatically be a lot more productive with your goals staring you in the face.

Realize that when it comes to setting goals and smashing them, the process is a continuous, complex one that is definitely worth it. It's the way you make your dreams happen. You just need to make sure you do not buy into any of these myths, and that you have the right tools. Then, your goals are a go!

## Tricks and Strategies for Goal Setting

Why goal setting? Because goal setting is a key to productivity. It is the process of figuring out the outcomes you want out of life in general, so that you have a solid framework to work off of, and you make progress. A lot of people are just like driftwood, floating, going nowhere exactly, even if on the surface you can see that they're working hard to make something of themselves. For the most part, they have no set destination. Does this sound like you? Well, if it is, we're going to have to fix that by setting some goals the right way. When you've properly set your goals, you're going to find yourself being naturally productive.

1. The pursuit is just as important as the prize. A lot of people don't think about the other stuff that happens as you make your goals real. It's a journey that will change you forever in one way or another. When you work on your goals, you will change. However, to paraphrase Tony Robbins, the goal of a goal is not about getting it. Still, about the person, you become in the process. This growth is where the real success lies. This growth will show you that you're capable of so much more than you think you could achieve.

2. Have the right timeline in mind. If you set a goal to lose 50 pounds in a month, then unless you're going in for liposuction, let me be the

first to heartily announce to you that you will fail hard and fail big. You need to keep your goals reasonable. Set goals that you know you can achieve within whatever time frame you have. If not, you will find yourself constantly disappointed with your lack of progress and overwhelmed by how far you have to go. If your goal will take longer than a year, then it helps to set benchmarks by which you can measure your progress, so you're more inclined to keep going.

3. Focus on the wanted, not the unwanted. If your goal is centered on what you don't want, then you're not going to get far. What is it you do want? Don't say to yourself, "I don't want this beer gut." Think, "I want to be lean, fit, strong, and have a healthy BMI." The great Robbins has suggested that whenever you can't figure out what it is you want, then you need to do something. Take actual physical action. He suggests going for a run while focusing on what it is you want.

When you constantly think about what you don't want versus what you do want, you are operating from a fear-based mindset. Change your mindset. I've already shared how you can do that. Become the person who feels the fear, and still goes after their goal.

4. Keep going even after you've hit your target. So, you made a million dollars. Congratulations! Don't stop there, though. Always set new targets to reach. This is how you grow. If you don't have a new target, then you're quickly going to find yourself wallowing in fulfillment and depression. It won't matter how lofty the goal you hit is. If you're unfulfilled, then you have failed in the biggest and worst possible way.

I'm not suggesting you should not take some time to enjoy the fact that you've nailed your goal. By all means, do! You must celebrate. Just make sure you think about what else you want next, make that your new goal, and keep at it. This is the way to stay satisfied with your achievements in life. It's not the goal you want. It's the growth. This is why you have new ones with each one you check off your list.

5. Don't fret about nailing our goals. I know you're probably confused by this one. After all, isn't the reason for setting the goal... the goal? The goal is not the goal. Growth is the goal.

The reason that we keep looking for what to do is that we feel the most alive when we're making progress. The journey, or the progress, is what matters. That's what life is all about. Growth means many things

to many people. Figure out what it means for you and aim for that. Seek growth, and you will become the best version of yourself. When you do, you'll realize even then, there's always room to stretch some more. That's the beautiful thing about life.

# CHAPTER 12

# Procrastinate Now, Regret Later

Surprisingly, the cost of procrastination only shows itself in the future. In a situation where you have few dirty clothes it won't be that much of a bother until you keep pilling them up week after week. Then you realize that there isn't enough space in your laundry basket to take more clothes.

Have you ever been in a situation where you are driving, and the police pull you over and walk towards you? How did you feel, especially when you knew you hadn't renewed your car registration due to prolonged delay? Well, that feeling you get is one of the costs of procrastination.

Was there ever a time you needed to do something important, but you procrastinated? Maybe you were supposed to deliver a work-related project, or you kept delaying payment for your insurance premium. If your excuse doesn't justify your actions or if you fail to act when you should, then you are allowing procrastination to take over.

Yearly, quite several Americans fail to file their taxes early enough and this has led to the loss of millions of dollars. You should also know that the majority of people that suffer from glaucoma blindness fail to apply their eye drops regularly.

Procrastination can cause you to miss opportunities, miss deadlines, and miss out on a lot of things. When you avoid a task that needs to be done, when you always use the "till tomorrow" phrase, and in the process sabotage yourself, then you are trapped in the ditch of procrastination.

The different ways procrastination can affect your life is undeniably obvious. The disappointing look you get from your friends when you miss a friend's get together or the "see me in my office" speech you get from your teacher when you fail to submit a term paper, makes it quite obvious that the result of procrastination doesn't feel good.

While some people always enjoy the last-minute rush just to accomplish a task, others often get caught up in over thinking the task and never get to take action. They both will always have to pay a high price when they constantly procrastinate, and it will become a difficult, bad habit to break loose from.

There is never a gain in procrastinating; rather, it is highly detrimental to your personal and business life. It can affect your business, which will cost you money when you stall those actions, or when you don't make the decisions you are supposed to make on time.

Failure to address issues that are a part of your finances will bring its cost—which will be a loss. You put things off and eventually don't get them done. Delaying will only limit and keep you from pursuing your financial goal.

Have you been contemplating saving some money monthly to have something for rainy days. However, you keep pushing it forward because you feel you are not breaking yet or there is still time? Or maybe you have some debt that needs to be paid soon, but you keep pushing up the payment week after week until you are embarrassed for not paying on time. Well, you will keep postponing if you don't summon the courage to start saving today.

These are the list that shows you how and what procrastination will cost you if you don't act fast. Let's take a look at some of those things.

## Loss of Time

The habit of stalling things or putting them off does cost us a lot of time. Some people should get their holiday groceries before the long queue at the mall or supermarket takes over. Still, with procrastination involved, they will have to wait till the last minute to get it done and end up wasting their time when it could have been avoided.

## Loss of Money and Incurred Debt

Lots of money can be lost when you procrastinate. When you don't book your flight early enough, you don't pay your fees when you should, or you don't buy a ticket on time, you end up paying more than the initial amount.

Also, people who find it difficult to plan meals or take their time to shop for groceries for their home, end up spending more money on dining out, buying take outs and ordering for food.

When you constantly avoid checking your account balance, opening your mail, or taking a look at how your income and expenditure are, it might create future problems that will make you spend more than your income and get yourself into trouble.

## Reduced Quality

It might sound funny but true that procrastination can lead to reduced quality. When you intend using the best decoration for a friend's birthday cake, but you don't start early enough due to procrastination, you might end up rushing the decorating, leading to a reduction in quality and not doing what you initially planned.

## Being Disorganized

When you start procrastinating on many things, they will pile up and clutter your home. Once you start being disorganized, it can lead to other factors that will do you no good. You start looking dirty, appear untrustworthy, and start feeling depressed from not knowing where to start from with your clutter.

## No Backup for Emergencies or Periodic Expenses

When you keep postponing to set aside some cash for the future, you might fall into an emergency and be stranded when you least expect it. Without emergency savings, debts can also be incurred, leaving you with the option of using credit, causing an addition to your monthly payment.

Saving for periodic expenses is also as important as saving for backup during emergencies. If you want to buy presents for Christmas. You don't buy them on time waiting until Christmas Eve, you will incur debt if you haven't saved up money or if the purchase price increases due to interest charges, you will end up paying more.

For people who procrastinate with home maintenance or repairs on their vehicles the result might lead to more expenses that can be very costly. If you need to fix a spoilt tap or a leaking roof but you keep postponing thinking you can still manage with its condition, what if water from the tap causes damage? You will have to fix the damage it has caused and also fix the roof or tap. So, your procrastination has led to additional expense.

## Worsened Health

Some people with an injury or illness will procrastinate going to see the doctor until the health condition gets worse or becomes critical. A worsened health condition is not only a risk to your life but also to other aspects of your life—you will have to miss work or school, and making up for these will be difficult.

A health condition might just be a minor one. Still, due to the unnecessary delay of visiting the hospital, it can cause serious complications.

The cost of procrastination is not only limited to the above, the list can go on and on, but I have carefully highlighted the very detrimental ones. Sometimes, procrastination can cost you more than one or even three of the above all at the same time. Still, they can be avoided when you adopt the tactic of counting the cost once you feel trapped in it.

Since we all know procrastination does come at a high cost and risk, why do we still neglect its consequences and continue it? Ask yourself if there are things you need to do that you keep postponing, does procrastination impact your life in any way, whether emotionally, financially or socially? And lastly, think of what you will achieve and how far you will go once you can start getting things done without procrastinating.

After answering these questions, you will be fully aware of the consequences of your actions when you procrastinate. Hopefully, that will put you into action. Inaction is the worst result that comes from procrastination, so once you feel you are in the loop of procrastinating, always recall what the cost will be and put the above into consideration. It will serve as a good antidote.

## CHAPTER 13

# Know the Enemy to Know Victory

Knowing what procrastination is by providing definitions is one thing, but knowing what procrastination is by examining what it looks like in your daily life is another beast altogether. The definition provided here is very simple: it is doing things that feel good at the moment, but that does not translate to long-term goals. For this definition to hold any water, it assumes that you have goals in the first place. Most people out there do. It can be anything from wanting to do better in life, to change your living situations, or even to become financially independent. These are all different types of goals, but they share one thing in common: they require hard work.

Procrastination then is a universal affliction felt by anyone who has a goal in mind. Even if the goal is the only subvocalization in the mind that nobody knows about, it is still a goal. Another word that fits here is desire. We desire fun and play (procrastination), but we also want some form of long-term change (requiring hard work). If you are stuck having fun and playing on your off hours, then you are robbing yourself of realizing long term commitments. Procrastination then is both a thief of time and a thief of self-realization.

An examination of your daily habits begins with a breakdown of the big things. The most obvious will be time spent sleeping, at work, or school. From here, you can move on to specifics. There are only 24 hours in a day, so it is crucial to figure out how these activities stack up. An example breakdown may look like the following. Most people will have very different breakdowns for any given day.

To simplify things, we assume full-time work in the example during a day in the week.

1.   Time spent sleeping ~ 8 Hours (33%)

2.   Time spent at work (including commuting) ~ 9 (37.5%)

Together, work and sleeping account for a whopping 70% of the daily time budget. This is some 17 hours in total that you have little opportunity to pursue long-term goals (assuming these goals are strictly unrelated to work). The other assumption is that work is engaging enough that long-term goals are impossible to work towards. This leaves another 7 hours to split up between leisure, responsibilities, chores and so on. This is where things get tricky. These 7 hours can be split in a seemingly infinite amount of ways over various areas.

Many of these activities are further split across the week, rather than a daily basis.

- Time spent towards personal upkeep (hygiene, bodily functions, eating)

- Time spent on home economy (chores, making dinner, buying groceries taking care of children)

- Hobbies

- Entertainment

- Socializing

- Exercise

- Work outside of work (seminars, acquisition of new skills, practice, etc.)

- 10. Countless others

The rest of the activity is left to you. The most important part is finding the amount of time that is considered leisure or your "own" time. In general, these are activities that fall below #4 on the list above. Everyone is different in this regard. Parents will generally have more time spent on children than non-parents. There will be a marked difference between those who work full time, part time and those who are unemployed. The more leisure one has, the greater the chances that they give in to procrastination.

The stereotypical image of an unemployment young person is someone sat at home doing nothing all day. Others who are unemployed treat their unemployment like a job, spending upwards to eight hours a day looking for work. Many of them also turn to the "gig economy" for extra cash by doing menial and specialized tasks for money on the internet.

## Bad Habits as One's Enemy

In terms of procrastinating, a bad habit is any habit that takes away from time going towards your goal. There could be several of these that you engage in throughout the day. These habits are also easy to identify. If an activity...

- Occurs almost daily for no definite period but can often take up an hour or more;
- Makes you feel good inside;
- Distracts you from the stresses of life;
- Is automatic in execution; autopilot-like;
- Gives you nothing in return after countless hours wasted;
- Simulates a sense of achievement without providing a proper return on investment.

This is not to say that any activity that makes you feel good is inherently bad. It's only when those activities outweigh your preferences for goal-oriented ones that there is a problem. Sex feels good and is a completely healthy aspect of human relationships. Porn addiction, out-of-control casual sex encounters, and masturbation addiction, on the other hand, are generally unhealthy. The porn addict is still missing out from a real relationship. The libertine may be looking for fulfillment in the partners he sleeps with, only to realize he can never find it.

Perhaps the biggest indication of a bad habit is time. Too much time spent doing anything relative to other activities is a sure sign of time being wasted. If it feels good while you are doing it, then doubly so. Most people reading this will already have an idea of what these habits are. Chances are you have identified them in the past but did nothing to affect change.

Still not sure what your bad habits are? Everyone has them; unless you are ultra-disciplined, then there are some activities in your daily life that you indulge in too much. We call this overindulgence, which is just a fancy way of saying doing nothing at all. Chocolate is an indulgence because eating it is pleasurable, but it needs to be modulated appropriately. Playing video games is an indulgence but playing them too often can cause you problems. Unless you are a big eSports star, then you probably shouldn't be playing eight hours a day.

Identifying some of these habits will be easier than others. The type of person you are will also determine how difficult they are to detect. Someone working full-time is less likely to be addicted to something that require a large time commitment, but they still may enjoy watching Netflix as soon as they get home. Far too many full-timers "clock-out" as soon as they get home and take relaxation to another level. In contrast, a student who doesn't work may find it easier to squeeze in time for their bad habits. These bad habits can be multiple and have a compounding effect on your time management. Even those without obvious addictions may suffer from the addiction of the "many". Having too many interests, obligations or artificial commitments.

# CHAPTER 14

# Paradox

What do the tasks you procrastinate on tend to have in common?

They all make you feel uncomfortable, anxious, or overwhelmed, don't they? Sometimes it's almost as if you're feeling actual pain when thinking about such tasks, right?

Well, that's because contemplating certain tasks does cause actual, physical pain. When researchers put people in fMRI machines and ask them to think about doing a dreaded task, the pain regions of the participants' brains light up, signaling that they're experiencing tangible pain.

When you're thinking about doing the taxes, you feel actual pain. When you're thinking about exercising after work, you feel actual pain. When you're thinking about writing your dissertation, you feel actual pain. No wonder so many of us keep procrastinating! Nobody likes to feel pain (except for the occasional masochist, I suppose). And what's our natural inclination when facing painful things? We shy away from them. Once burned, twice shy. Of course, people want to avoid and put off certain tasks — they hurt us.

While some people can think about difficult tasks with no problems, procrastinators think about certain tasks and immediately start feeling bad. Procrastinators tend to have deep emotional scars that lead to having negative associations with certain tasks. It's everybody's fault that everyone feels this procrastination-causing pain. Still, it's our responsibility to learn how to handle it and function despite it.

Keep this in mind next time some smart-ass tells you something along the lines of, "Just do it already. What's the big deal?" Well, it's not that simple. And everyone who's ever struggled with procrastination knows that it's impossible to "just do it." That's exactly our problem — for whatever reason, people can't just do it. But I digress…

Coming back to experiencing pain when contemplating certain tasks, it may very well be that you're unaware of this pain in your day-to-day life. That's because it tends to happen unconsciously.

As an example, you may make the conscious plan to study after school today. At night, when going to bed, you may realize that you didn't do it. Whoops, what happened? Your unconscious mind steered you away from the pain, that's what happened.

To bring back our little analogy, the monkey urged you to run away from what feels painful and toward what feels better. You may have watched some TV, had a nice dinner, and gone out for a beer with your buddies — activities that feel good. That's the monkey unconsciously and automatically guiding your behavior away from pain and toward pleasure. It will, of course, take a fair amount of awareness on your part to see these patterns operating in your own life. And now for the good news. Research shows that there's an easy way to get rid of the pain associated with certain tasks: Just. Get. Started. As soon as you start engaging in a task, the pain evaporates. Barbara Oakley, an expert on student procrastination, explains in her book A Mind for Numbers:

"People procrastinate about things that make everyone feel uncomfortable. Medical imaging studies have shown that mathphobes, for example, appear to avoid math because even just thinking about it seems to hurt. The pain centers of their brains light up when they contemplate working on math.

But there's something critical to note. It was the expectation that was excruciating. When the mathphobes really did math, the torment vanished."

Intriguing, isn't that so? The agony is in the expectation, not in the real execution of a feared task.

If you need help from negative feelings brought about by feared errands, you can either stall, which essentially defers the torment, or you can simply begin on the assignment (more difficult than one might expect, however methodologies are coming). When you begin, the torment dissipates.

What's more, this close moment help with discomfort isn't the main thing that is going on when we begin. Other research shows that the minor demonstration of beginning intensely moves our impression of the errand and ourselves. Timothy A. Pychyl, a main dawdling scientist, clarifies in his book Solving the Procrastination Puzzle:

"Shockingly, we found an adjustment in the members' impression of their undertakings. On Monday, the feared, kept away from task was seen as upsetting, troublesome, and terrible. On Thursday (or the extremely early times of Friday morning), when they had occupied with the errand, they had maintained a strategic distance from all week, their observations changed. The appraisals of errand trouble, and disagreeableness diminished altogether... indeed, numerous members offered remarks when we paged them during their very late endeavors that they wished they had begun before — the assignment was fascinating. They figured they could make a superior showing with somewhat more time."

When you begin, you understand it's not close to as terrible as you suspected.

The assignment isn't as overwhelming, horrendous, troublesome, or upsetting as you've envisioned. Hell, it's in reality sort of fun and fascinating. Furthermore, hello! You're not as apathetic and inefficient as you suspected. You can do this! You can be taught and complete things!

Even better, you're presently effectively taking a shot at your assignment and are most likely gaining extraordinary ground. Gaining ground feels incredible thus your temperament, good faith, and fearlessness get another decent lift. Out of nowhere, you're feeling peppy, positive, hopeful, and certain about yourself — you currently have some ground-breaking positive energy on your side.

The little demonstration of beginning makes expanding influences and gets under way an entire apparatus of self-sustaining upward spirals. As you begin, torment leaves, discernments change, and you begin making energy.

It resembles Newton's law of inactivity expresses: "An article very remains very still and an item moving remains moving."

It's everything about changing from non-doing to doing.

That is the thing that tarrying boils down to: moving from non-doing to doing. A huge piece of beating tarrying implies showing signs of improvement at doing that switch.

Fortunately, you become better and better at doing the switch every time you do it.

Each time you conquer the persuasive surface pressure and move from non-doing to doing, you improve at it. Each time you figure out how to begin on troublesome errands, you develop that muscle of blasting through obstruction and doing the main priority whether you feel like it or not.

Everything tallies here. You either fortify the example of unnecessary deferral, or the example of beginning and beating obstruction. Now you may interject, "But Nils, this is exactly my problem! I just can't get started!"

You're right. Getting started is simultaneously the root of the problem and its solution. If you can't get yourself to begin a task, if you can't resist the pull of the monkey, you'll end up procrastinating. If you can get started, on the other hand, procrastination gets nipped in the bud.

To overcome procrastination, you need to get better at getting started, vetoing the monkey, overcoming resistance, handling negative emotions — call it whatever you want.

Ultimately, most of the tactics in this guidebook will help you with that in one way or another.

For now, let's look at five specific short-term strategies that you can start using immediately.

TRY THIS: Focus on The Next Step, Not the Next Thousand Steps

A major reason many of us procrastinate is because we're overwhelmed.

It's an uncomfortable feeling that is sure to get our monkey out of its cage. The monkey wants to run away from the uncomfortable feelings and, as a result, we become resistant to the task and experience an urge to do something more enjoyable.

Because of that, we tend to be especially vulnerable to procrastination when facing big projects, which are naturally challenging and overwhelming. All those options, unknowns, and uncertainties are almost unbearable for the monkey, which is why it tends to run rampant when you're contemplating large projects. Where should you even start? What's the priority? What's a reasonable deadline? What are all the things that still need to get done?

It's almost impossible to get started if all those overwhelming thoughts are swirling around your head.

The key to overcoming this type of procrastination is to simplify things by breaking the project down into small, actionable steps.

First, create a list of all the things you'll need to get done. Second, create a plan — which tasks are you tackling first and in which order? Third, stop worrying about the steps further down the list and start focusing only on the very next step. Fourth, just get started on that very next step.

Quit stressing over completing everything. Quit stressing over all the things left to do. Quit agonizing over what's still to come. Simply continue concentrating on the extremely following stage.

Theodore Roosevelt once stated: "I long for men who make the following stride as opposed to agonizing over the following thousand stages."

Furthermore, Mark Twain appeared to concur when he stated, "The mystery of excelling is beginning. The mystery of beginning is breaking your complex overpowering undertakings into little sensible assignments, and afterward beginning the first."

Along these lines, start concentrating on one thing in particular: the following noteworthy advance. And afterward begin on that. Try not to allow yourself to stress over the following thousand stages — that is a surefire approach to get overpowered and dawdle.

John Steinbeck, a Nobel Prize winning writer, clarifies it impeccably: "When I face the ruined difficulty of composing 500 pages, a wiped out feeling of disappointment falls on me and I realize I can never do it. At that point, step by step, I think of one page and afterward another. One day's worth of effort is everything I can allow myself to think about."

Try not to permit yourself to look excessively far ahead. One little and significant errand is everything you can permit yourself to mull over.

Inch by inch, life's a snap; yard by yard, just getting by can be a struggle.

Presently, reasonable warning: This strategy isn't as simple as it might sound. It requires exertion and determination. You'll need to effectively occupy your concentration from the mind-boggling parts of a venture, at that point pipe it onto the following significant advance.

For whatever length of time that you're ready to maintain your concentrate tight like that, your monkey will murmur along without upsetting you.

# CHAPTER 15

# Value of Decision Making

So, we've looked a little at where you are and how you got here. Now we're going to examine where you want to be. Don't forget through this that whatever we want, it must be in line with our deep-seated values and beliefs.

If we are to make changes, we must decide to change. That may sound a little crazy on the face of it, but it can be explained by this thought. Whatever you do today, wherever you go, every single thing that happens is going to happen because you decided that it would. Remember, you have the choice. You are the one driving the bus.

If you decide to do nothing, then that too is a decision. It is, of course, not a very good decision. It's very likely that deciding to "not decide" has been a great influence on where you are today. It means that you are allowing life just to happen. You are allowing yourself to be carried on the tides and refusing to take control. This may well mean that someone or something else is dictating what happens in your life. Is this really how you want it to be?

Every day, we all make hundreds, if not thousands, of decisions without even realizing it. Many of these decisions are automated, unconscious ones, which we have made so many times before that they become part of our being.

Try to make more of your decisions consciously, as opposed to unconsciously. You are in control of every single thing you do. Your entire life and everything around you are how it is because of the decisions you made in the past. Yes, this is going to be hard work, but if we are to change, we must do something different and work harder at being more conscious.

Left to our own devices, many of us humans would just sit around and do nothing. It's only when we are dissatisfied with things that we decide to change something. That doesn't mean that we are all lazy. What it means is that we must have a reason for doing something. There must be a benefit to making a change.

It is a fact that we have to have a reason for everything we do. In many cases, though, the things we do are unconscious. Many of the things we do are by the force of habit. Habits that we formed because we wanted to think something or feel something, or do something. And we did it repetitively until it became a habit.

If there must be a purpose to every action we take, try to think about the following as you go through your day:

· What am I hoping to achieve by my next action?

· How will I benefit from what I'm about to do?

· What alternative actions could I take?

· How would a different action influence the outcome?

· How will what I'm about to do force me into other actions in the future?

Procrastination is the fine art of putting off until tomorrow what you should do today.

As an example, imagine you have half an hour to spare and are pondering whether or not you've got time to mow the grass. As you've only got a small lawn, this could be done easily within the time available. Do you quickly get the mower out of the shed and cut that grass? Or do you leave it until tomorrow?

Of course, we all know that the best thing to do is to mow the grass today. Because tomorrow, it may rain. And it may rain the next day too! It won't take many days of not mowing the grass for it to become more of a task than it originally was. If left for a few days, it's possible that instead of the job taking less than half an hour, it's going to take a whole hour.

That decision to put off mowing the grass has stacked up another task for you in the future. That's another task that you have to deal with on top of the ones that were going to be there anyway.

This is one of those examples where it would be easy to be lazy. Instead of mowing the grass when we had our half hour to spare, it would be very easy to make a coffee, sit down, watch a little TV, or phone a friend for a chat. I know that in my own life, I've had to train myself to do things straight away. Even the smallest things are important. Don't let anything get away. It's doing the small things right away that helps to train us. Instead of going down the same old lazy, well-trodden path across the meadow, we start to become accustomed to walking a little bit more in the long grass.

Even though we know it, we still allow procrastination to be a major problem by allowing ourselves to do the same old things and getting the same old results. Recognizing that we are running these auto-response scripts is key to interrupting them and making different decisions.

Just taking some positive action by making a different decision, even on the smallest of tasks, is a massive step to helping to overcome those old habits and replacing them with new, dynamic ones. By starting small, we begin to train our brain into new ways of thinking. Do it over and over again. Make sure that you never put off something that you could do right now.

It is worth remembering that every day, we are all making many decisions. A decision is a choice. If we choose to, say, drive to the beach, then that is a decision that we have made. If we choose to have roast potatoes with our dinner this evening, then that too is a decision.

We know that probably 80% of our choices are made automatically based on what we have always done. Choices about what time we set the alarm. Choices about what we wear, what we eat and drink, etc. We make choices about how we spend our time, where we work, what we do with our leisure time, who we socialize with, and so many more. Every single one of these is a decision that we make.

Every single thing we do every single day is driven by the choices we make. Our decision to drive to work is something that we might have done consciously when we were late one day, but now, it might be just playing that same old auto-script that no longer serves us. Driving to work may not be necessary if you only live ten minutes' walk away.

When making decisions, try not to make any life-changing plans when you are under lots of pressure. Or, if you are under pressure, find a way to relieve that a little before making any commitment to change. Although the very concept of Procrastination to Power is based on moving, it is imperative to move in the right direction. Moving in the wrong direction will almost certainly lead to frustration and annoyance.

Failing to make any real progress in my quest for a better life didn't surprise me too much. I put it down to making half-hearted decisions. I had simply gone a little down a certain road with a new project just because I could. I did this with such little commitment that it was doomed to fail from the start. All I succeeded in doing was wasting time.

We all have such a short amount of time on this earth, why would anyone want just to waste it?

If we're going to make good decisions, we must try to consider the outcomes. In my role as a coach, I help people to look into the future and see how their life looks from a year or so away, or sometimes even further. We examine different outcomes for different possible choices. I ask my clients to imagine themselves in the future. I ask them about what has happened in that year. Are they still happy with the choices they made? What could they do differently to get different outcomes?

If you have several choices, and you always do, try writing down all of the options, then project yourself into the future and look at the results of each option. Take some time doing this.

Try to put yourself into the future and see how you feel about the results. Try to experience the whole of being there, in that future. Close your eyes and go to that place in your mind. Does it feel right? Does it look right? What did that choice bring you? What was unexpected about the results?

When you're happy with what you feel about your choice, look back from the future and examine what you did to get there. Looking back from a year into the future, what were you doing last month, three months ago, six months ago, etc. What steps did you take to move from

Procrastination to Power? What is different about you now? How did you make the changes that you wanted to make?

Deciding to change something or to do something different is the first thing we must do, but that's not enough. Yes, we can do something different today. Still, to make that stick, we've got to keep doing it over and over again until it becomes second nature. If we don't work hard at it, the risk is that we overcome procrastination today, only to fall back into our old habits again tomorrow.

The good news is that to be someone different, we can begin by doing something different. It's the doing that is going to make the change. It's a sure fact that simply thinking about change will not make the change. The only possible way for anything to happen is if you make something happen. You can think about making changes and say to yourself, "Yes, I'll be more dynamic and more motivated." Still, if you don't actually do something there and then, your next sentence may well be, "I'll start first thing tomorrow."

In those moments of creating my birthday card to myself, I wasn't only preparing to do something different. I became something different. At that moment, I became an author! I was no longer some guy thinking about writing a book. I was an author, and it felt so good. I generated that feeling by doing something. I made that birthday card for myself. I took action, and that action is what started the ball rolling.

Initially, when someone suggested I make a vision board about what I wanted, I was very skeptical. I didn't believe that doing childish things like sticking pictures onto pieces of card would do me any good. I was a fully grown man with three grown-up kids of my own. I didn't need to be playing around with such things at my age. What I had decided to do, though, was to do something different. I went along with the idea of making this vision board. Why not? I had spent years trying all sorts of things to get me moving, and I hadn't moved at all. I had nothing to lose. Doing the vision board was quite fun, and it certainly helped me to internalize my vision for the future. Anything you can do to sway your likelihood of achieving your dreams is worth a go. Don't dismiss anything. As the saying goes, "Don't knock it 'til you try it!"

The reality is that every decision or choice you make will have some kind of effect on you. All of our choices have an impact to a greater or lesser extent. Many of these will be insignificant, but some will have lasting consequences.

## CHAPTER 16

# Planning and Priority Management Techniques

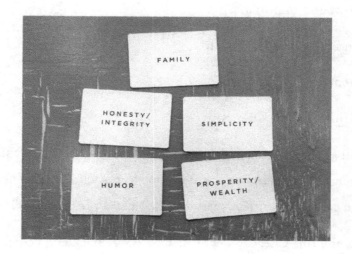

O
nly now that you know how to overcome procrastination, you can take care of how to organize your actions better, and to do so, you have to do four additional steps.

Step 1: How to Set Priorities

Dwight D. Eisenhower was the 34th president of the United States, a five-star general, the founder of NASA, and the first Supreme Commander of NATO. It would be an understatement to say that he was a driven man who knew some strategies for success and productivity. Eisenhower had a tool that he used to set his priorities and plan how to use his time efficiently. This is widely known as the Eisenhower Matrix. It looks like this:

Everything on Eisenhower's to-do list would fall into one of four categories:

1) Urgent and Important

2) Non-urgent and Important

3) Urgent and Unimportant

4) Non-urgent and Unimportant

Things that were Urgent and Important had to be dealt with first. These were things of high importance and value to Eisenhower that needed to be taken care of in a timely matter or that had a pressing deadline.

In daily life, this category might include your check engine light being on, a presentation at work two days from now that influences your success at work, or a sick child in need of medical attention. These would be listed in the "Quadrant One." Because these tasks need to be taken care of first. It is the next three categories that often trip people up and have cause them to get bogged down, working on things that are of little or no importance to themselves.

In the Second Quadrant, Eisenhower would list things that were Non-urgent and Important. This is the category that needs the most planning and attention. It is the category that will help you focus on what you value the most and help you achieve your long-term goals. In this category would be things like exercise, time with family, home and vehicle maintenance, further studies, self-improvement, short-term and long-term planning, money management, volunteer work. These are the things that focus on self-improvement, relationship strengthening, and planning for the future. These are the keys to our sense of fulfillment and success.

Two main issues may be preventing you from spending enough time in this category. One is simply not knowing what is important to you or what you want from life. If you decide what you want, you can work towards that goal. If you are unsure, you will end up simply "treading water" and not making progress in any specific direction. The other issue is being so caught up with urgent business (important and unimportant) that you have no time to work on what you value most. It is important to note that if one plans well, life will be less filled with urgent business, and life will calm down. For example, good planning and budgeting will prevent the time- and energy-consuming stress of a personal financial crisis. Regular home and vehicle maintenance will help prevent an urgent repair need.

This brings us to the third quadrant, that which is Urgent and Unimportant. These are thrust upon us: a favor, an interruption, a trivial meeting, things that often distract from that which is important. This category must be trimmed wherever possible. Some things can be delegated to others. If a friend asks a favor that you are not suited for, perhaps you can point them in the direction of someone more able to help. Other tasks in this category can be delayed or even eliminated.

Learning how to politely decline additional responsibilities that add no value to our lives can help immensely with urgent, unimportant tasks.

The final category of the Eisenhower Matrix is the fourth quadrant, that which is Non-urgent and Unimportant. These tasks simply do not need to be done and can be eliminated or, at the very least, pushed to the very bottom of the to-do list. This category would include notorious time-wasters and other traps that procrastinators often fall into.

Step 2: Eliminate Distraction

For a procrastinator, it is particularly important to eliminate the distractions; for this, it is useful to go further into this point. When we eliminate those things that are neither urgent nor important to us, we have more time to focus on the things we want and need to accomplish. I want you to picture a familiar scenario:

You sit down to work at your desk. You glance at the clock and think confidently, "Three hours! I have plenty of time." Then your phone rings, an email "dings" into your inbox, and a group text from your kickball team brings in seven new messages. You look at the clock again and suddenly, 3 hours have become 30 minutes. Where did the time go?

It has never been more imperative that we eliminate distractions that rob us of precious time! Specifically, we can be more aware of the time we are wasting on social media or web-browsing. There is even software that helps track and limit time spent online. If it is possible for your situation, you could unplug from the internet entirely while you tackle offline tasks.

As far as the smartphone goes, a small step that just about everyone can benefit from is to turn off notifications. These are rarely helpful, and they are a constant time waste. Another way to eliminate distraction is to work with your phone in flight mode and activate it only when you take a break. You could even get your phone off for a time. 'Unplugging' is almost unheard of today, but it is both liberating and helpful in increasing our productivity.

Another form of distraction is clutter and disorganization. It has been shown scientifically that messy environments increase our stress level and affect our ability to focus. If you clean up your work environment, there will be one less thing to worry about when you are trying to focus on what is most important to you.

A last form of distraction is emotional distraction. Some people in our lives seem to bring nothing but drama and negativity. These "emotional vampires" tend to suck all of the positive energy out of our lives. If we can ward off these vampires, we keep our emotional energy in reserve and avoid being bogged down by unnecessary, distracting negativity.

Step 3: Completing Tasks

As a modern society, we have been told that multitasking helps get things done. Your internet browser probably has multiple tabs open at any given time, and your phone is most likely beside you and interrupting at intervals even as you read this. This has become the norm; it is how we live. But have you ever tried to text and drive at the same time? There is a reason it is dangerous. Doing multiple things at once means that nothing gets done well or efficiently. Learn to do one thing at a time and always carry it to completion. Do not start another task until the first has been completed. You can start by practicing small things like loading the dishwasher, cooking, writing emails, etc. Let the momentum and satisfaction of a task completed carry you onto bigger, more important tasks.

If at first, you struggle to stay focused, chose a set timeframe, or even set a timer. For example, you can work at a task for 10 minutes, take a break, and then continue at the task at 10-minute intervals until the task is completed. As this becomes easier, you can train yourself to focus for longer periods.

Step 4: Planning (to Beat Procrastination and Increase Productivity)

Once you have utilized your Eisenhower Matrix to see which are the most urgent and useful tasks for you to focus on, you need to use this information to make a to-do list for each day. Before you go to bed, write a to-do list for the next day. You can start small and build. If you did not complete a task, write down why it wasn't done and reschedule it. Strive to finish everything on your list. As you become more comfortable with the system, you can write more detailed lists with specific time goals. (e.g., 10 AM – 11 AM respond to emails, 11 AM – 12 PM phone calls, etc.)

Find ways to make your life more efficient. If there are any aspects of your life in which you could save some time, it's about time you started doing it. Saving yourself some time in some areas will leave more time for you to attend to the other, more pressing matters. For example, if you were to invest 2 or 3 hours one day during the weekend to prepare your meals for the rest of the week, you'll save so much time during the rest of the week because you're not busy cooking your dinner or your lunch, which leaves you more time to attend to other matters. Look at all the tasks you have to attend to and see where you can group similar activities so you can tackle them in one go. Increase your productivity by minimizing the time spent working on activities individually.

Another tip for planning to increase productivity is to think about when you are at your most productive. Are you a night owl or early bird? Different people are productive at different times. Some people feel more motivated in the morning; some feel that way in the evening. If you want to make the most out of your productivity streak, find the times when you feel the most energetic and productive, and choose that time to make the most of your tasks schedule. If you focus best in the quiet hours after midnight, it isn't such a good idea to attempt a complex task first thing in the morning. Go with what works best for you.

When Procrastination Is Not the Problem – Other Issues Which Look Like Procrastination: Not Knowing Where to Start, Perfectionism, Inner Conflict?

It may happen that the typical dynamics of procrastination are not the cause of inaction.

Not Knowing Where to Start

In this case, instead of choosing instant gratification over a delayed reward, a person delays action because they are overwhelmed by possibilities and does not know how to begin. In this instance, you might continually research options without ever starting towards your goal. It can be extremely overwhelming and stressful when you feel like you're being faced with multiple choices, and you don't have the faintest idea where to begin. When dealing with important, life-changing decisions, it can be even more stressful, especially with the pressure of knowing you have to make the right choice.

Sometimes it is the excess of information that confuses the ideas: especially today that it is so easy to find any information online, it can be difficult to organize and choose which ones are suitable, at a certain moment, for us.

In this case, it is better to start and course-correct along the way only. A simple and effective way to overcome this indecision is to set a deadline and start. It is better to make changes along the way than to waste time waiting for the perfect moment. Small steps are better than no steps at all. You don't always need to have all the answers to everything before you begin. Remember that our old friend motivation often shows up once we've started on the journey. Along the way, dig into that motivation to keep you going, remember why you started in the first place. Doing something is better than doing nothing at all, and this is something your future self will thank you for. Even if you make mistakes and stumble along the way, hey, at least you reached the end and finished it!

## CHAPTER 17

# Understanding Procrastination and the Value of Time

The person who procrastinates this way will put things off and act like everything is under control and all is well. They've got this. And for the time being they believe they do have all matters in hand even though this road has been well-traveled. For some reason, there have not been enough shake-ups to cause the person to make any changes as of yet. Not enough close calls or massive failures. Luck has been with this person for at least up to this date and time.

These are people who procrastinate because they do not understand the concept of time. This type of procrastinator will overschedule the number of tasks or an unreasonable length of time for each task to do in a given span of hours, always thinks that they have plenty of time to do those tasks. In contrast, a person who has a good concept of time understands how much can be done in a given portion of a day and will only schedule tasks to fit into that portion of the day.

Often the person who over schedules too much because of a poor concept of time might have an enabler in their life. Or, they may have several people who cover for their wackadoodle schedules and activities. This kind of thing is widespread among politicians and other people who have committees to delegate things to.

When the person who over schedules themselves realizes what they have done, they become anxious and work extremely hard almost every day. These people as a rule, rarely have time for any fun activities or relaxation. They are always pushing the envelope because they are always behind. These people almost always plan too much into each day because their concept of how much can be done each day is unrealistic about the amount of time that they actually have.

This type of procrastinator might actually benefit from making their schedule in the morning as always, but to also plan in a fun activity in the schedule for a specific time during the day. This fun activity should be right in the middle of all the work. Taking time out to take a breather, might actually help this person. When they see the time allowed for fun, this might trigger the time allowed for the other activities they have planned that they never get finished.

Instead of being discouraged about unfinished projects, this procrastinator might start planning for the correct allotment of time to do things they might actually get done. This in turn will produce less stress and anxiety and less procrastination.

Time management must be taught to this type of person who procrastinates. Understanding how much can be done in a given time frame is very important. Looking at a task or project and having help from a mentor to break the task into smaller more manageable pieces that can be completed in specific allotments of time is an excellent first start. If this person has just a little mentorship to help guide the process, then this person can learn the time value of what they usually ask of themselves. And how they often set impossible goals.

The opportunity to change by breaking down a task is a great way to have a fresh start not to procrastinate and put things off because the job seems too hard and the time constraints are too narrow. Break the job down and extend the time constraints actually to fit the job. If that is impossible, try breaking it down at least into digestible bites that are equal and more doable than before.

This gets stated over and over throughout this guidebook but breaking down tasks into manageable pieces is the key to breaking the procrastination cycle. Often, the person who is procrastinating doesn't understand time or the magnitude of the task. By having smaller chunks to work with, the time is also breaking into smaller pieces as well — less of a task for a little less time. Everything becomes less so therefore it seems more natural.

Perception of how big a situation is maybe a key for the procrastinator. The point of view is changed so the habit of procrastination becomes more comfortable to change. We begin to work on the entire mindset behind what we are doing. Sometimes when we look at things from a certain point of view, our mindset actually changes, and we can tackle the problem from a different angle.

Another solution to the time factor and procrastination may be to get a planner. This can be an electric planner or a pencil and paper planner. Critical times and dates should be put in the planner first and then other things filled in on the daily as they come up to be completed when they are due. There usually is a place for a daily or weekly list on a planner and this might be helpful as well.

Good old-fashioned honesty is required of a person and the way he or she handles the time available each day. A person has to be able to look in the mirror and examine what is going on when there are way too many tasks scheduled for the time allotment.

Is it true that a person who has poor time management does not care enough to manage their time better? Some people believe this is true. Most psychologists who have studied procrastination and time management say it is more like a Superman or Superwoman type of syndrome where the person believes they can actually get all the things done in the time they say they can even though the rest of us may look at the list of tasks and the time frame and shake our heads.

This requires a great deal of honesty on the part of the procrastinator to look and see that these tasks will not fit into the time frame allotted. Perhaps if the projects have been started sooner or the projects were modified in some way then maybe. But not as they are right now. This list is impossible for the time frame. And this person needs help.

An intervention to help this type of procrastinator realistically look at the time and how much can be accomplished in an hour or 30 minutes would be helpful. This person needs to practice. Interestingly, on this particular trait, the younger the person, the harder it is for them to be convinced. Why? Young people are invincible. Older people are more like, "Yes, you got me. Now please show me a better way on this. I'm exhausted." There is hope for people who have no concept of time.

## Self-fulfilling Prophecy of Negative Thinking

The power to think positively is powerful indeed. And the power of negative thoughts is also powerful as well. The saying goes, "if you believe you can or believe you can't you are probably right."

A person who procrastinates often gets stuck in negative thoughts. "I can't get things done because I have too much to do. More often than not, procrastination is the result of being overwhelmed., By and large, the habit of procrastination is reinforced by feelings of being overwhelmed.

A person who procrastinates can let himself or herself be talked into waiting one more hour or one more day to start any task. And one that has been pulled way down, will listen to the negative thoughts that say, "I am going to fail anyway."

Negative thinking can be a barrier to anyone's success. Any new habit you are trying to create or any old behavior you are trying to break, letting the negative thoughts seep in will get you down. A positive mental attitude or a PMA is famous in so many circles and groups for the success of the people in the group. But it's true. Having a right attitude and chasing away the negative.

Push negative thoughts back down and if there are negative people around you who are bringing you down in your quest for self-improvement, you need to think very carefully about who you are socializing within your free time. If it is someone at work, keep it professional, but give them as wide a birth as possible and you become the ray of positive sunshine to accomplish your goal.

Follow your heart and make the call. Write the email and go after what you want. Do you know how many actors, athletes, and musicians were told at one time or another they were not talented? Michael Jordan was cut from his high school basketball team. We've all heard that story. Poor Judy Garland was put down every day of her childhood. But she knew she was a star. What about Meryl Streep? She was also told she had no talent. Hmmm. Lose the negative talk and risk. Don't listen to anyone who puts you down or tries to plant a seed of negativity. They are not looking out for your best interest. When you feel down, the chances of procrastination increases. Push the negativity back and don't let it near you.

Negative thinking also includes finding problems in exterior things – the traffic, the noise, the irritating coworker, and anything else you allow to bring you down. Let those things go and keep your focus on your goals and your priorities. The negative thoughts are distractions that drag us down from the goals we are trying to accomplish.

## How Changing Your Thinking Can Change Your Future

Every thought you think at any given time is planting seeds for the future. When you think positive thoughts, you will move in positive directions. When you think in a negative thought pattern, you will move in a negative direction. This sounds like common sense, doesn't it?

Your past thoughts have brought you to this reality you call the here and now. And the reality you are creating for tomorrow is your thoughts of today. You are literally deciding your future by the way you are thinking and by your actions today. Your future is in your control by your thought patterns right now.

There is a mind-body connection between stress and our ability to connect the dots for ourselves. What is meant by that is our minds and our bodies need to be working together in sync in order for us to make decisions. When we are working in top form and have good habits, we are able to make good decisions that are good for us and those around us.

It's not that people who procrastinate don't care. Sometimes it's that their lives are in such disarray it's difficult to sort through the situation to get into the feelings. The person cannot afford to care because at the moment he or she is just surviving. Most things are being put off or are not being taken care of at all. Bills, license tags, grocery shopping, and more are only done when they absolutely have to be done.

The mindset has to be changed. The disarray has to be cut through by someone who cares, so the person is able to sort through their feelings and be able to make sense of their daily routines. They will need to start small and work their way up to larger tasks on the daily and weekly levels.

How does this affect procrastination? By thinking positive thoughts and visualizing a positive future, he or she begins to choose positive acts for themselves. Visualize getting up and making the bed, making that healthy breakfast. Then when you get to work, taking care of tasks as they arise. Making time to exercise at some point during the day and staying active each evening. Choosing new thought patterns will help to choose a new healthier future free of procrastination.

## CHAPTER 18

# The Good and Bad Things
# about Procrastination

Procrastination is an inherent human reaction to different kinds of stressful stimuli. Therefore, it is neither good nor bad. It only becomes such depending on the situation. Thus, these are the important things to remember about the good and bad things about procrastination.

## The Benefits of Procrastination

The thing is that our society is so obsessed in being productive and efficient that we end up loathing procrastination. In fact, there are many adages that discourage people from procrastination. Although procrastination has a negative connotation, its definition per se refers to the body's defense mechanism when faced under a lot of stress.

There is such a thing as positive procrastination and it refers to putting off things in order to perform "mental percolation" which is to gather one's thoughts to get a clear view on what needs to be done. However, it is important to take note that the benefits of procrastination are only applicable for active procrastinators. Active procrastinators are people who put off tasks because they need more time to plan. They are not avoiding tasks but they are taking steps albeit small to complete their tasks. Below are the benefits of procrastination.

•	Better work under pressure: Not everyone can work well under pressure but active procrastinators can flourish if they are given time constraints to finish their tasks. They spend more time in planning so when the deadline is nearing, they can work efficiently.

•	Allow time for ideas to flourish: Active procrastinators are great in conceptualizing ideas as well as making them flourish. Moreover, procrastination can also help push frustration away because the ideas have already been tested even before it was implemented.

•	Relaxation is beneficial in terms of productivity: People who tend to procrastinate before starting their tasks tends to be more productive compared to people who are always working all the time. The reason for this is that procrastinators have more time to relax so they are not at risk to sleeping or burning out in the workplace. Putting things off may cut the time that you have to complete a particular task but you will end up more equipped to handle tasks after a taking a break.

•	Procrastination can cut down work: When completing a particular task, people have this ability to expand or shorten the project depending on the time that is allotted. Procrastination is beneficial in cutting down work so that the tasks are intended directly to achieve the goals. This removes people from doing frivolous or redundant work.

•	It offers the opportunity to plan ahead of time: Productive procrastination is very proactive because most people tend to sit with an idea before they act. This means that before they decide to take a break, they have already planned what they need to do one they decide to go back to work.

Procrastination is a trade-off and we are constantly doing it in whatever things that we do. As long as we are procrastinating in a reasonable way, it is really trivial that we are putting some things off.

## The Disadvantages of Procrastination

While positive procrastination is beneficial, negative procrastination encourages people to make flimsy excuses in order to avoid doing their tasks. This leads to a lot of problems in the end. In most cases, the disadvantages are often experienced by people who are passive procrastinators. Below are the many disadvantages of procrastinating:

• Poor morale: Procrastination always results to things that are undone or poor quality and this often leaves people the feeling of guilt on not doing things that they ought to have done. This also leads to having poor morale particularly in the workplace.

• More distractions: Unfinished jobs often leave a lot of clutter which also affects the efficiency. The presence of clutters can also cause a lot of distractions.

• Reduced productivity: Compared with active procrastinators, passive procrastinators accumulate their jobs without any idea on what to do. Thus, the urgency might crop up the same day and they cannot handle anything thus everything crumbles down.

•      Unhappiness: People who procrastinate tend to become unhappy even if they work in the most highly motivating jobs. They are also branded by people as lazy or lacking of any interest in anything that they do. Employers usually do not trust procrastinators with important projects.

•      More stress: Procrastination is a defense mechanism for people to avoid stress but putting off things can lead to more stress. This is especially true in the work setting wherein it is impossible for you to avoid your tasks and putting off your tasks meant that you have limited time to finish everything.

•      Deteriorated health: The stress that accompanies procrastination can lead to deteriorated health. Stress can cause different types of diseases including headache, inflammatory diseases and autoimmune responses.

The many disadvantages of procrastination are the reason why it is so crucial for people to learn how to deal with them.

Research has shown that the group that is most likely to fall into procrastination and be chronic procrastinators is students; there are plenty of adults who are chronic procrastinators too. Here we are not talking about someone who will put off a project on occasion because they are busy or they just do not feel like doing the work; we are talking here about the people who are chronic procrastinators, the ones who do this action so often that it is now part of their personality. They may not pay their bills on time, they will wait until as late as possible to work on deadlines, and nothing is ever done on time with these kinds of people.

While being a procrastinator and falling behind on things on occasion is not that big of a deal, it can sometimes turn into something worse. On occasion, procrastination is seen as a good thing because it will teach you a good lesson about getting things done on time and sometimes you can learn a little creativity to get the work done faster next time. However, if you are a chronic procrastinator and this becomes a regular habit, it is going to become a part of your lifestyle. This means that it is going to impact many different aspects of your life, including your stress levels.

There was one study that was completed in 2007, that found at the beginning of a new term, students who were procrastinators were sick less often, and they did not have to deal with as high of levels of stress compared to those who did not see themselves as procrastinators. On the other hand, by the time the semester ended, the ones who were procrastinators were sick more often and had much higher stress levels.

This is just one example of how procrastination can take over your life and impact your health. It can also take over some of your social relationships as well. For example, if you keep putting off some of the tasks that should be done now, you end up placing a lot of extra burden on those around you. When working as part of a team, any time that you turn a project in at the last minute or even late, it places an even tougher time limit on others to get the work done faster than before.

Those around you are going to become more resentful because you add more work and pressure on them.

Do procrastinators act differently than others?

As mentioned before, procrastination is not usually going to be a huge problem. It is a tendency that many people will have to deal with at one point or another. You may actually be sick one day and decide to take a nap rather than getting your work done or you just cannot figure out how to get started so you wait until later. And as long as you do not let this become a habit that you do all of the time, it is not a bit deal.

However, when procrastination starts to become a chronic condition, it could have a big impact on your daily life and it can become a big issue. In these cases, it is not just because you are having issues with time management, it is becoming more of a maladaptive lifestyle.

As a non-procrastinator, you are someone who is able to focus on the tasks that need to get done. They are not as concerned about social esteem as much and they often have a stronger personal identity compared to others. Often, they are going to be conscientious to other people, meaning they want to get the work done as soon as possible so that no one else has to worry about their part or wait around for it. These people may also have some other great personality traits such as personal responsibility, persistence, and self-discipline.

On the other hand, those who are procrastinators are going to be different. They will probably feel a low self-esteem because they are always late on things and this affects how others are going to perceive them. They may not have the motivation to get things done and they are not good at managing their time to get the work done. They may spend their time on time wasters rather than getting stuff done, which will often stress them out more than the task at hand should.

The good news is that even if you are a chronic procrastinator, you can make some changes to your lifestyle to see better results. Procrastination may be a habit that is hard to break, but just like any habit that you may fall into, it is one that you will be able to beat and overcome. You simply need to have the motivation to make this happen and you need to put in the hard work as well.

## CHAPTER 19

# Five Tips to Simplify Your Life

I f you are a routine procrastinator, you probably feel overwhelmed and underappreciated. Here are five quick tips to help simplify your life.

## Number One: Honesty

Be honest and have integrity. Always. If you can't share the truth, then keep it to yourself. But under no circumstances should you actually make up a lie and tell it. Or then again set out to deliberately delude somebody. That is the speediest method to muddle your life that I am aware of. Do what you state. State what you do. On the off chance that you lie, you need to recall what you stated, and to whom. What's more, recollect whether you advised something other than what's expected to another person, and afterward attempt to shield those two individuals from conversing with one another. Discussion about confused!

Some may fight of holding the reality, when it is "gawky" to tell all that you may know, is up to this point misleading. I would need to concur. In all honesty talking, that is a deceptive practice. In any case, from an absolutely "down to earth" perspective, saying "less" is regularly the way toward a less perplexed life. In any case, accepting, obviously, holding reality will do authentic evil.

By then there is the matter of the "harmless distortion" as individuals like to put it. Aunt Gertrude asks with respect to whether you supported the multicolor sweater she cautious sewed for you at Christmas (that horrifying thing beginning at now stowing interminably in the most noteworthy openings of your storage room). Do you say "I believe it's the ugliest thing I've whenever seen," or do you discover a comment that will save her sentiments. I pick the last referenced, yet don't go over the edge. Take the necessary steps not to state, "I respect it. I wear it each possibility I get!" That is likely going to set you in a place of wearing the defect to the going with family assembling. Or on the other hand possibly, locate within ground, for example, "Each time I take a gander at it, it urges me to recall the total you love me." Problem comprehended.

## Number Two: Declutter

If you want simplicity, then less is more. Less to take care of. Less to clean. Less to protect. Less to store. Less to worry about. Much, much more time to simply "be."

On the off chance that you have amassed a ton of "stuff" during your life – congrats on your bounty! Be that as it may, it will overload you, and muddle your life. In the event that the errand of cleaning up appears to be overpowering, simply recollect how to eat an elephant: One chomp at once. So, pick a room or region to spotless, set your clock for

25 minutes, and go at it. Rehash until done. You will be astounded at how much "lighter" you feel.

## Number Four: Routines

Make schedules that smooth out your life and stick to them. Schedules could incorporate choosing your closet for the following day and hanging it where it's anything but difficult to put on toward the beginning of the day, or setting up the espresso pot so it's all set first thing when you get up, or washing the dishes once per day whether you feel like it or not, or covering every one of your tabs around the same time of the month. There are handfuls more I could list, yet ideally you get the thought.

Schedules are intended to improve, not to trouble. Try not to make a standard that adds work to your life. Just make one that will at last spare you time and inconvenience. Cluster things together instead of doing them piecemeal (with stops and starts that sit around), or plan your tasks in a single enormous circle around town, as opposed to a few separate outings. Try not to be excessively inflexible about it. Leave a little adaptability for what "life" will toss at you.

## Number Five: Introspection

Do some contemplation day by day. Either with a diary (which I suggest), or simply some tranquil "think" time. Offer your thanks, vent your dissatisfactions, do some critical thinking, or whatever rings a bell. On the off chance that you utilize a diary, you can intermittently survey it to search for patterns. In the event that they are sure, you can fortify them. In the event that they are taking you off course, you can make careful and educated move. On the off chance that you discover entanglements and troubles that repeat (that you might not have acknowledged you had), you can start to issue unravel, and improve your life further.

## The Five H's of a Well-Balanced Life

For your thought, here are five H's of a decent, profitable, glad, and "non-procrastinated" life. It was initially four, yet I as of late included a fifth. For you Management Theory buffs, make certain to peruse as far as possible (however don't begin there – it will ruin the amazement).

Health

Placing health in the main space is an easy decision. Truly, before family. On the off chance that you don't keep up your own wellbeing, you aren't a lot of good to your family – or any other individual besides. It resembles the guidelines you get on a plane to "put your own breathing device on first before helping others."

Wellbeing incorporates body, psyche, and soul. It's a comprehensive arrangement. It implies getting enough rest, eating right, directing energizers and depressants, being fittingly dynamic, taking enhancements and physician endorsed meds normally, watching feelings of anxiety, not letting things or individuals bug you, and doing things you appreciate consistently. Everybody is unique, so you should tweak to accommodate your circumstance.

It doesn't damage to have a day by day check list. Prescription – check. Went for my stroll – check. Tuned in to some music I love – check. Et cetera. Once more, you have to redo to suit your specific needs. Furthermore, don't be modest about requesting what you truly need. On the off chance that you don't ask, by what means will others know?

Home

Home methods various things to various individuals. To me it implies things and individuals that sustain and bolster my center presence. My close family, my genuine house where I hang out, my day by day propensities, etc.

This is the place I put exercises, for example, investing energy with my loved ones, keeping up around the house to make it perfect, agreeable, and safe, and dealing with all the day by day tasks that permit life to stream without any problem.

There should be food on the table, and a rooftop over my head, clean sheets to set down on, agreeable garments to return on my, etc. It additionally implies chipping away at those "connections" that make your life exceptional and one of a kind. You can't disregard these things for long, in any event, for a "respectable" cause.

Honor

I utilize this as a shorthand method to remind me to "respect" my responsibilities to other people. In this class I fit my commitments to my work, my congregation, any clubs or associations I have a place with, etc.

Here is the stunt. You should perceive how much "respect" will continue your wellbeing and home, and keep it at that. Try not to exaggerate these commitments, regardless of whether you feel "blameworthy" for not doing some of them (e.g., I should go to that Christmas Party yet I don't feel like it, and so on.). This is the place the exercise in careful control gets crude for a few. A significant word to learn here is "no."

## Harmony

I love music. It is my obsession. To state I "need" music in my life is a genuine articulation. I have to hear it out, play it, believe it, etc., every single day of my life. For you, you may discover your agreement in nature, or playing sports, or painting, or cooking, etc. Whatever "reverberates" with you is your congruity. I could have called it "euphoria" yet that doesn't begin with H!

In finding your concordance, you will discover your quality and manufacture your fearlessness. It goes past what you do at "work" and causes you express your actual self. It is imperative to discover time for your happiness, regardless of whether just somewhat every day.

## Heritage

This is my fifth, and as of late included H. It's actually about amazing quality and heritage. This is tied in with deserting something for people in the future. Many, numerous individuals do that with their kids, and there is nothing amiss with that. For me, I need more. I need something of hugeness that I made, that will outlast me.

This is a significant part of your life, yet you clearly can't chip away at it until the initial four H's are leveled out. This carries me to the incredible "uncover."

Synopsis

I think you'll see that it's simpler to keep up parity and center on the off chance that you have a little mental helper device to recall what's significant. What's more, it will surrender you a leg on your New Year's goals!

Presently, get out there and compose your own form. I've given you the formula. You should simply locate your own fixings and blend well!

# CHAPTER 20

# The Pareto Principle

In conjunction with the notion of prioritizing tasks in your everyday schedule, there are times when you will be tempted to work for longer hours. This is what most people do with the hopes of compensating for time lost. There are folks who also have a habit of working for longer hours since they consider it as the best way of being productive at work. Sure, this might sound like a brilliant idea to get things done. However, according to Vilfredo Pareto, a celebrated Italian economist and mathematician, this is not the best way to work productively.

The Pareto Principle was introduced by Vilfredo Pareto (Linehan, 2019). This principle is also called the 80/20 rule. Through Pareto's analysis of the land ownership in his country, he came to realize that 80% of the land was owned by 20% of the country's population. Following his conclusion, he applied his mathematical principle in other settings. Over the years, the principle has been accepted as the "universal truth" considering the fact that there are various settings to which the principle applies.

In any business setting, the Pareto Principle dictates that there is a disproportion of inputs and outputs. Take a look at the total profits that a business gain. 80% of the profits are contributed by only 20% of the customers. In the healthcare industry, the principle also applies. In this case, you will find that 20% of patients are responsible for 80% of healthcare spending.

There are also day-to-day examples that can convince you of the fact that the Pareto Principle indeed applies. How many applications do you have installed on your smartphone? Many, right? It is not surprising that you only use 20% of these applications. The same goes for clothes that you have in your wardrobe. Chances are that you only wear 20% of these clothes 80% of the time.

## Evaluating Your Tasks Using the Pareto Principle

According to the Pareto Principle us, 20% of your efforts will often lead to 80% of the results that you obtain. Wait! Does this mean that you should be lazy? Certainly not! It only means that you should understand that for you to be productive, you don't have to work for longer hours. What you should do is eliminate activities in your schedule that will only waste your time.

When evaluating tasks using the Pareto Principle, it is important to review your to-do list to see whether it features your most important tasks. Consider whether the tasks on your list are urgent. Determine whether there are certain tasks that take up too much of your time before you complete them. While doing this, you shouldn't forget to review whether some of these tasks require delegating. More importantly, ask yourself whether the tasks listed are important.

By abiding by the Pareto Principle, you will find out that your to-do list has a lot of junk that you can eliminate. Most of the time, we tend to prioritize specific tasks with the perception that they are important. The reality is that they will not make a huge difference, if any, if you avoided them completely. Ideally, you will realize that you will spend more time on what is important and matters to achieving your goals.

## Identifying Your Prime Time

Undoubtedly, there are specific times of the day when you feel that you are more productive than at other times. Maybe you find it easy to work in the morning from 9 am to 11 am. It could be that you are more energetic in the evening. Depending on your prime time, you should aim to use this time to work on 20% of your goals or tasks for the day. Keep in mind that you would have listed these tasks based on their importance.

## Identifying and Eliminating Time-Wasters

Distractions will always be there when you try to use your time productively. Nevertheless, this shouldn't deter you from finding practical ways of eliminating them. Before that, it is important to identify these distractions. What are some of the time-wasters that prevent you from focusing on your job? Your list can include activities such as phone calls, emails, social media, unplanned visits and visitors, hunger, etc.

Using the Pareto Principle, you can easily get rid of these distractions. The 80/20 rule will mean that 80% of the distractions you are facing are from 20% of the sources you have in mind. Now, from your list, you can pinpoint those that divert your attention the most. For instance, social media notifications can affect your performance at work if you spend most of the time going through the notifications you get. You might end up spending as much as 2 hours scrolling through these pages. Unfortunately, you will only realize this after you have wasted a lot of time. Such disturbances should be dealt with as soon as possible. There are times that handling distractions that hinder you from using your time wisely.

The 80/20 rule not only helps you in finding ideal ways of using your time wisely, but it can also be applied in other areas of your life. Once you notice that the principle is helping you live a productive life, you should utilize it in everything that you do. Whether you are paying your bills or engaging with friends, the Pareto Principle should guide you in knowing how to focus on what's more important.

# CHAPTER 21

# Strategies That Can help You Change

I f you are going to overcome procrastination, it is important that you understand the stages that you have to go through to break this habit. This uses the stages of the change model that helps people learn how they can get rid of self-destructive behaviors.

It is very important to know the stage of change you are in currently. This ensures that you use specific strategies that will help you to effectively take you through that stage and into the next level of personal recovery. If you fail to use strategies that are specific to your stage of change, the chances are that you will stall your recovery. It explains the reason why so many people who have gone through rehabilitation have not been able to s shake off successfully their old self-destructive had.

## Stage 1: Pre-contemplation

This is a stage that is characterized by a lack of awareness of your problem. During this stage, you do not have any intention to act in the foreseeable future in an attempt to fix your problem. In other words, when you are at this stage, you are not ready to change. It is mainly because you have not accepted that you have a problem. You are simply in denial.

One thing that you have to understand is that if you are at this stage, it is important that you have factual information about your procrastination habit. This way, you will be able to understand the real consequences of your actions so that you are better equipped to make informed choices about whether or not to quit your habit of procrastination.

You could also discuss your problem and concerns with a therapist or a friend who can offer you accurate feedback on how your procrastination habit affects you and the people around you. They will actively help challenge your denial so that you can work towards recovery. The worst thing is allowing your procrastination habits to cause pain and even death to the people you care most for. When you start working on your recovery, you will be inspired to get back on the right track.

## Stage 2: Contemplation

Now, you are already aware that you have a problem and you intend to do something about it. However, the problem is that your intentions at this point are still vague because you do not have any idea what to do about it.

At this stage, what is going through your mind are the do's and don'ts of continuing the self-destructive behavior, giving up altogether. In other words, you are at a stage in which you are undecided. It is important that you speak to a professional therapist concerning your thoughts on how the change will come about.

You should ensure that you use your therapist to bounce off the merits of continuing your procrastination habits or even quitting altogether so that you can make an informed decision. Seeking the help of a professional assures you that you will be able to think through all these issues more productively. It also ensures that while you do that, you do not pass any judgments so that you accept yourself the way you are.

## Stage 3: Preparation

This stage involves you having a plan on what you intend to do so that you can deal with the problem of procrastination. At this point, you have decided that quitting the habit of procrastination is the way to go and are acting. One thing that you have to do is to gather adequate quality information on your procrastination change program and join people who have struggled with a similar habit and have been able to overcome.

## Stage 4: Action

When you are at this stage, you start acting on your plan or course of action in an attempt to overcome your procrastination habit. In other words, at this point, you are already changing. It is, therefore, important that you surround yourself with people who can actively help facilitate your attendance to your procrastination change program.

Ensure that you can engage the people that mean a lot to you, such as your friends and family to help support you through the process. Such group sessions not only help you share your problems with others but also inspire you to work towards addressing the issue of hearing what others have gone through because of their procrastination habits. Such support is important in helping you keep track of your progress.

## Stage 5: Maintenance

At this point, you are no longer procrastinating. However, you continue to take the necessary actions that you need to ensure that you do not slowly allow procrastination back in your life. In other words, what you are doing is continually reinforcing change, support, and encouragement to keep going.

You have to realize that, when you are at this stage, the temptations may loom but not as strong as they used to be. This means that you have to enlist the support of your close friends, colleagues, and family to keep you accountable for your actions and decisions. They will ensure that you remain on the right track to recovery so that you not only consolidate but also internalize the change so that it comes naturally.

Note that there are so many things that might try to undermine your progress. But you have to remember that you are not yet completely out of the woods and hence it is not time for you to be complacent. Trying to convince yourself that you have been so good and just one procrastination will not make a difference is a recipe for disaster, and you will find yourself right back at the pre-contemplation stage!

One interesting fact that you have to bear in mind is that many people often go through several cycles of change before they can successfully overcome their self-destructing habits. Think about alcoholics, smokers and others who after trying and failing many times, they come out the other side free of their habits! In the same way, you can take your procrastination habit as a sport or weight loss plan that you have to work hard to get where you are going eventually.

## Stage 6: Termination

This is the point at which procrastination has been eliminated and is no longer a problem. It is important to note that for some people, getting to this stage can be tricky because they risk relapsing to their old habits. In other words, you will need to stick to the maintenance stage indefinitely.

Additionally, the amount of time and condition to overcoming procrastination varies from one individual to another. Therefore, while there are those that will overcome their behaviors fast, there are those that will take a significant amount of time to get there finally. Nonetheless, the longer you stick to your plan by sticking to positive habits, the easier for you to keep going, and the better you get at overcoming procrastination.

## Experiment and Reassess

One thing that is important to note is that there is no single cure for procrastination. This is mainly because procrastination is a complex problem in which different people will benefit from varying strategies and solutions.

This means that there is no one right way to stopping procrastination. Instead, the best approach is one that helps you deal with the issue by first understanding your habit as much as you can. Then you can try applying various approaches and solutions to it until you find one that works best for you.

Start your day on fire

If you are going to enjoy everything you do, you have to start the day on fire. When you are pursuing your dream, you will go through seasons of struggle and victory. One day, things are very exciting to you, and the next day, you are bored and are tempted to procrastinate. To overcome the temptation to procrastinate, it is important that you express your deepest desire, purpose, and passion. If you are going to work hard at attaining your goals, then you have to be willing to live in your passion.

Yes, you want to see your business succeed or career take a new direction. To do this, you have to say the words that set you on fire and then take a step further to light the fire in your career, business, and team. In other words, you have to put passion first before practicality.

Four years ago, a friend of mine leaped faith to start their own business. It was a huge step, and she started by writing her vision, mission, and value statements. Each year, she read through them and made a couple of improvements, but that did not seem to be enough. Then I advised her to start reading them aloud each day, first thing in the morning, and things began to take root.

The points are:

Vocalizing

When you start reading your goals and dream out aloud each morning, these hits both sides of your brain. Notice that the left side of the brain is logical whiles the right side if more emotional and motivational. In other words, the left side of the brain justifies what you tell it and tries to create negative resistance. Therefore, by reading your goals, dreams, or tasks aloud, what you are simply doing is unifying both the right and the left side to work together towards realizing those dreams.

Practicing daily

It is important to note that motivation is more like exercising, means that the more you work out, the more you become stronger and fit. It also goes for stirring up the passion within you each morning. Think of today as the most important day of your life. Simply make a fresh start and turn towards the right direction.

## First things first

According to Stephen Covey, the author of "Seven Habits of Highly effective people," you have to be willing to do the first things first if you are going to achieve your goals. This means that you begin every single day with the things that matter most. In fact, during the very first two hours of the day, spend it pursuing positive and nourishing ideas. In other words, rather than starting the day with the newspaper, emails, gossip, and social media, among other things, start it with what makes your dreams come true!

Start your day by reading your goals and mission out loud. This will make you feel dynamic, energized, and will stir the internal fire burning within you to come alive on the outside. You have to go the extra mile to feed that fire as often as possible.

Look out for the things that come in to let the fire out of your day and avoid them. These are the things that cause you to want to procrastinate on those dreams. It may be a customer that is always complaining, a coworker that is distracting you with meaningless stories and gossip or a traffic jam that makes you get to work late among other things.

Realize that it is time to pay attention to your vision. Think of yourself as a Marathoner, if you stumble and fall, you get up, dust yourself, take a deep breath, refocus, and start running in the right direction. The truth is, it does not matter how many times we make mistakes, procrastinate, or fail to meet deadlines, what truly matters is being able to pick ourselves up quickly and work fast on recovery.

One thing that comes to kill your fire is procrastination. It tells you that your goal is what you have to do rather than what you dream of being. It tells you that you are what society wants you to be rather than what you want to be. It causes you to forget your mission and dreams. It pushes you to start resisting and hating what you love doing in the first place.

## CHAPTER 22

# Choose your Workplace and Time

Sometimes self-control feels like an internal thing. If you're struggling to ignore distractions and focus on important tasks, it's not just your brain that's holding you back. Sometimes the space you're working in can be the very reason that you're struggling so much.

When I first started to attack my self-control, I was completely focused on productivity. I went to my office and cleared everything out. I made it the whitest, brightest, most minimalist space possible. I kept it clean, pure, and free from anything other than work.

After about a week, I started feeling a lot sadder. I was getting things done, but I was still unhappy. My productivity increased, but my level of passion or intrigue decreased.

While I might have managed to strip myself of any added distractions, I also took away the chance for me to connect to a work space that made me more passionate.

Don't make the same mistake that I did when I first started. Minimalism can help some people, but going too extreme could mean you're left feeling empty and bored. What might exist in your workplace now isn't working just right. However, don't assume you have to match the clean aesthetic you're seeing everywhere at the moment. Your workspace should be reflective of your personality with an emphasis on encouraging productivity.

## CREATE AN APPROPRIATE WORKPLACE

Your physical work space should be an area that inspires you to cultivate success. Productivity comes from what you're feeding your brain. If you're in an environment that leaves you feeling stressed out, there's no way you could expect to find productivity.

Consider the layout, design, and overall feel of your workspace.

I like to incorporate cream, pale pink, and green into my workspace to provide me with a relaxed feeling while still staying in a neutral zone. Gold and wooden accents provide me with creativity and inspiration while staying connected to nature.

I'm obsessed with lighting different spaces as well.

As an experiment, grab three different types of lights and go into a dark room. The first light should be a basic lamp with an average lightbulb. The second is a lit candle, and the third is a colorful light. If you don't have one, that's perfectly fine, but find a different light source to experiment with. Alternate between each light as its own source in the middle of the room. Notice how everything looks different. It will change the way that your eyes perceive things around you.

You can also experiment by lighting the opposite ends of the room with this source and notice the way they change the color of the wall. I highly recommend everyone invest in colorful lights for their homes. You can buy remote-control bulbs and LED strips to place around your home at a relatively inexpensive rate. These lights increase my creativity and help me to transform my space. Sometimes casting just, a blue light over the room provides me with a different kind of focus than a relaxing candle.

If a workspace is too dark, it can leave you feeling unmotivated and maybe even sad. Choose natural lighting above all else to have this continue to power you throughout your day.

When the lighting is bluer, you might be more focused. However, too bright of a light could strain your eyes, especially if you're staring at a screen all day. If you're working from home and looking for a more peaceful environment, stick to warm orange and yellow lights. These could help mimic sunlight to keep you feeling energized and soothed.

The color of the room is also important. If you have control over what the color might be, pick blues, purples, and other cool shades to keep you relaxed and focused. While something like neon yellow and bright orange seems energizing, they can overstimulate you and heighten your anxiety too much. Even when you don't have much influence on the color of your workspace, you can still bring in items that could potentially fill the room with that color.

Make sure to allow some elements of nature in to keep you connected to the space. If you can, fill your windows with plants and at least have one at an office you don't have control over. By giving yourself the ability to have this refreshing element, you can stay more connected to your space when you might feel distant from yourself as a human.

If you're sitting at your desk pumping away at the machine all day, it's easy to begin to feel like a robot yourself.

Nature elements keep you grounded and remind your brain that you have fun and freedom readily available. If you are the type of person to kill houseplants easily and don't trust yourself with a plant, you can include pictures of nature. Having photos of you on vacation and with friends is a great reminder of fun times, fulfilling that need for motivation as you're chugging away at your computer.

Have snacks and unlimited water when you're working for long periods of time. Be cautious with snacks; we mentioned at the beginning if you're creating a distraction-free zone not to include any. If you can, keep them in a cubby or locker at work rather than right at your desk. The same goes for your home office. You should have them within walking distance, but not necessarily arm's reach, or else it could be too tempting and lead to mindless eating later on.

## USE PRIME HOURS

As we mentioned earlier, you should have a period of time where you track your time. To recognize where you're giving effort, you should first understand how your schedule works with your natural abilities to work. We all have internal clocks that can affect the way our mind works. Some people are morning people and do really well with waking up early and starting their day right away. Others do better when they can stay up late and have the peace of the night to focus. Some people work best in the middle of the day when they've had time to relax in the morning but don't want to have to work all night.

After you've tracked your time, it will be easier to see when your most productive hours were. Look back over your schedule and see at which hour and on which day you were able to accomplish the most.

Consider the setting as well. Sometimes it might not be the hour, but the location you were able to get the most work done in. When you're planning your week out the next week, you can more easily plan around days that will be more productive. If you're using the prioritized tasks method of planning, you can still reserve special times to chunk these high priority tasks together. For example, you can have mini to-do lists specifically for those peak hours and then plan accordingly around those moments for the best outcome possible.

There are many factors that determine when and why you are productive. Sometimes it's what you eat, who you are around, or even the weather outside. Track all of these aspects to see not only when your peak moments are, but how you can try to cultivate those peak moments other times.

For example, I found I was very productive Thursday nights. I had the entire weekend to look forward to and only one quick work day to go. I had put pressure on myself to finish fast from what I had procrastinated throughout the rest of the week.

This excitement and this pressure are what motivated me the most. I had to ask myself, "How can I create these emotions other times?"

One thing I did was made sure that I had something to look forward to every day. I created fun routines to remind myself to get the work done quick so I could have a stress-free night. One night maybe I made homemade pizzas with my family. Perhaps another night I treated myself to my favorite restaurant. Some nights simply having a movie to watch later was enough to give me something to look forward to. I would use my excitement throughout the day to stay focused on my tasks because I had something to look forward to. Thursdays were still a little more productive than the rest, but that is when I knew I would be able to effectively catch-up with everything I wasn't able to get done.

You can find your peak productivity hours the more that you pay attention to identifying how you spend your time. What are you doing that is making you less productive, and why do these circumstances keep you from completing tasks? What helps keep you motivated and encouraged to get the rest of your important accomplishments done? Eventually, you will be able to find a productive flow state, working effectively in between your mental ups and downs.\

## CHAPTER 23

# Stay Optimistic and Live in the Moment

Above all else, your attitude is going to be the most beneficial tool you have in this process. While you might not be the most productive person now, that doesn't mean you can't be in the future. However, your perspective might be one thing that continues to hold you back.

When you realize you're your own biggest enemy, it can be a pretty big epiphany.

I hated my life at one point. I woke up disappointed every single day. I went to bed bummed out that I didn't do more. I hated all the tasks that were ahead of me and I loathed having to do anything at all. I had things that I wanted to achieve in life, but I wasn't actively working towards them. I was just trying to glide by, miserable that I had to put in any effort at all. I was always stressed, the world wasn't fair, everybody was out to get me. I had to pay bills, I had to make people happy, I had to impress others, and I had to do this all for myself – a person I barely even liked!

The stress ate away at me. I got worried that I wasn't being successful. I had fears over not being able to pay bills. I was constantly consumed with doubt and fear. I always wondered why I couldn't ever get anything done. I was always procrastinating, stressed, and worried. Then it hit me. It was this very stress that was keeping me held back. It was the anxiety about getting something done that would be the biggest roadblock in the way of me actually getting said thing done.

It wasn't my work that was hard. It was the mentality that I had about it.

That was one of the most challenging things to break through.

Being a positive person doesn't mean that you're blind. I always resented people who were optimistic for that reason; I thought they were just turning away from the real world.

I thought, "Well, don't they know how many people are suffering in the world? Aren't they aware that many bad things happen all the time? Don't they understand that life is not fair? How can you be optimistic in such a cruel world? In a place where animals are harmed, people are suffering, war is constant, and hunger is everywhere? How can you be happy? How can you be positive?"

Once I learned what my negative thought patterns were, I began to really investigate them. When I asked myself, "What's there to be positive about?" I started countering with, "How does negativity help any of that?"

When you start looking back on notable figures in the world who have really changed things for the better, many of them had one thing in common: they had a positive outlook.

Nobody gets up, stands behind a podium, and makes an incredible and (truly) moving speech by talking about how everything sucks, and nothing matters. Sure, that could be true. Nobody's saying that perspective is wrong. I'm not telling you that being happy is good and being negative is bad.

The only one that you are hurting when you have a negative perspective is yourself. Believing the world is a bad place and everything is terrible does not solve problems. While it might not necessarily be false, it's not getting anything done.

Being positive does not automatically fix problems either.

However, it does help to alleviate that pressure that is holding you back from accomplishing things.

Let's say you're in your final stretch of the college semester. You have two projects to finish and one big exam to study for. One project is easy and you actually enjoy doing it. The test is extremely hard, and you don't know how you're going to pass. The other project that you have to do is very time consuming, so while you have an idea of what to do, you don't necessarily know if you're going to have enough time to get it done.

I want you to picture now two students in the exact same situation.

One student is negative. They don't understand why they have to do this stupid project. It's not really helping them learn anything and it seems like just a waste of time. The teacher is probably not even going to look it all over. Everybody else in the class is going to do better. They're probably going to fail their other exam, so what does it even matter? What's the point of doing anything at all. They're just going to go to college graduate, and then move on. Who knows if this is even going to help guarantee a good job? Why bother?

The other student thinks, "Well, I have nothing left to lose. If I do get a bad grade on this, at least I'll know what I'm good at and what I'm bad at. If I completely bombed all my finals this year, that just means maybe I should reconsider my major next semester. A lot of my idols have failed in the past, and they never gave up. The only thing that I have to do right now is study. Nothing else is going to make this easier for me. I'll be fine if I just make it through. I only have five more days left."

Which student do you think ended up doing better with their project? Neither student was necessarily wrong. It's not about being wrong or right. It's not about having the best perspective. It's about having the perspective that's going to make you the most productive in this process. To really put your focus on something you need to be present in the moment. You need to be paying attention to everything that's sitting right in front of you. If your thoughts are on the future and what's going to happen, then you're not going to be able to focus on the task. If you're constantly thinking about all of the regrets you have and how you should have started sooner, that is also not going to finish the task. The only thing that will complete the task is you and putting your attention towards it. That is why positivity can be one of the most beneficial things for this process.

# BE POSITIVE TO INCREASE ATTENTION

Some studies suggest positive emotions enable our ability to focus better. Stress can keep us distracted and worried. It's hard to pay attention to important things if you're afraid of the results.

So now that you know life is all about being positive to be more productive, how exactly do you do that? When everything is seemingly terrible, what is it that can put a smile on your face?

For me, one of the most important and effective things that has dramatically changed my life is practicing gratitude. Again, positivity and having gratitude are not being blind to the bad things.

It's simply not letting those control your life.

Having gratitude means being aware of the good. You don't have to necessarily celebrate it and be extremely happy or passionate about it. It's simply the acknowledgement that you have privileges, benefits, and great things in your life. For example, let's think of an easily gratifying situation.

Pick out one of the wealthiest celebrities that you know.

They have fame and positive attention from people. They have a massive house to live in. They have all the clothes, shoes, purses, cars, and makeup you could ever want. They seemingly have it all, and it's easy to see what they have to be grateful for. You can look at the material things they have such as their clothes and their house. You can look at greater things such as money and fame.

For example, a celebrity and a rich person - they have a lot to be grateful for too. Now imagine that they lose the ability to walk. Maybe they get diagnosed with cancer. Perhaps they discovered all their friends and family hate them.

It's not necessarily the fact that any of these situations is bad, but those material objects that we mentioned being grateful for would come into play and help balance things out. What I'm trying to point out is that no matter what the situation is, rich, poor, healthy, unhealthy, there will always be things to be grateful for. There is not one singular situation that is best or necessarily better than any other.

All we have is what we have.

You have to make the most of that. Rather than thinking about all of the things that you want to get, hope to get, should have gotten, and could have worked harder for, you can focus instead on the things that surround you now.

LIVE IN THE MOMENT

Living in the moment is all about being mindful and aware of the present.

This is essential because it's usually fear that keeps us so trapped in our own mind. Fear usually stems from unrealistic situations. It's a vision of the outcome. Even if you're sitting in your apartment and you hear a loud noise in the other room, that fear comes because of the unknown. That loud noise could have been your cat jumping off of a table. That loud noise also could have been five intruders accidentally knocking something off your desk. Fear also comes from things that are out of our control. Let's say those five intruders do walk into the room you're sitting in and they're staring at you.

All of a sudden, you don't have any control anymore because it's you versus five people. The fear sets in again.

We fear things that are out of our control from our past. These are moments in time that have been taken away from us, and we can no longer get back. Not only can we not reverse the clocks and make things turn out in our favor, but they have affected things in the future that we still have no control over as well.

Self-control is all about living in the moment. This is the core of the book. This is the meat of what I want you to understand.

## MANAGE STRESS

Stress has so many more effects on your mentality than you would even be able to fathom. Stress can also have physical effects on your body.

On one hand, think about how you might clench your jaw and your fists. You might keep your shoulders tense and maybe your legs shake. Your stomach could hurt because you're always keeping it tight and wound up, and your head feels like somebody hit it with a brick. Unmanaged stress can lead to even greater and more serious issues. You could have chronic anxiety or depression. It can also trigger other mental health problems that you already have.

Stress could even lead to a heart attack, diabetes, or stroke, if not managed properly. Of course, other things can come along with that, but for the most part you want to recognize stress is not just something mental. It's a chemical process that occurs in your body. Cortisol is a hormone that is released whenever you are stressed. It makes your heart beat faster, your focus becomes more alert to present danger, and you are ready to use your fight or flight response.

# CHAPTER 24

# Understanding Who You Are and
# What Your Purpose Is

We are all created with a specific purpose in life. We are tasked with finding a meaningful purpose that holds a deep meaning to the future of our lives. Our purpose is something we must find within us; it is not a process with which can be created from nothing. By uncovering the purpose of your life, you will be able to create a life that is worth living and enjoyable. You may find yourself asking, "What is my purpose in life?" You can find your purpose by identifying what you are passionate about and then incorporating it into a joyful and happy existence. To fulfill this need to find your purpose, you should start by exploring 2 things:

1.  Examine the things that you like to do
2.  Examine the things that are simple and easy for you

By doing a large quantity of work, you will be able to develop the talents that are needed to live with purpose. Not a single person can jump straight into talent and be successful. Consider the foremost precocious musical talents; they still have to work hard on their craft, no matter how talented they are. However, if you feel like you are upstream without a row, then you should consider finding a new passion and purpose. Although it is hard work, it still should be easy work that is enjoyable.

- Examine the explicit qualities that you enjoy expressing the most throughout your day.

Start off with asking yourself some questions like, "What 2 qualities do I hold that I can utilize to express myself to the world?" I like to express compassion and love to others in the world.

Next, proceed to examine these questions a bit more, "What 2 ways do I enjoy expressing these qualities towards others?" The two ways I express these qualities to others within the world are to help empower women to take actionable steps for their families and lifestyles.

- Create a statement of your purpose in life

Take time to sit down and hash out the statement that you wish to express as your purpose for life. In a world that is living with the highest of good, you would see everyone who lives with the vision that they have of their life. Then you would be able to envision those that are living a passionate, and purposeful life. Finally, the last step is to mix these 3 statements for the purpose of a transparent plan which can help you live a purposeful life.

A purposeful life plan could read similar to this: "Empowering and inspiring action in others to create a healthy lifestyle and live their dreams."

- Follow the guidance from your inner knowing - what do you hear from your heart?

What would you say if I informed you that you have your own inner guidance that is ingrained in your psyche? This inner guidance is similar to GPS. It can direct you where you should go and how to feel about the journey. Your internal GPS is similar in comparison to the external GPS which you would find within your phone or car. It will help you direct the car in the right direction, which is the same thing that your internal GPS will do for your life.

When driving in your car, you can use your GPS to help you get to a specific location. However, it initially will start by locating the current location that you are in. Then it will offer you the directions that will lead you to your destination. Your internal GPS is designed to do the same thing only in a completely different way. It starts with locating how you feel about the current situation then it directs you on how to change those feelings to suit your lifestyle better.

The navigational system works hard to figure out what process is needed for you to be able to locate your appointed destination. While heading in a specific direction, you will begin to receive signals that come in from satellites that are located in multiple different locations within the atmosphere, and it then will calculate the position you are in precisely to help you with aiming your direction the route you need. Next, it will plot the course that is ideal for your travels.

- Decide on the directions that you wish to go to.

All you need to do is process the direction you wish to take your vision and then work out the exact directions that will take you there. By locking in your vision for your life, you will be able to set the goals that are needed, write affirmations, and create a visual image. This will help you to take appropriate actions that will bring you closer to your end vision.

With each visual image you place within your mind, you are "inputting" your preferred destination into your mind and establishing a path that you will take during your travels. Every single minute you use towards reaching your specific destination will provide you the purpose that you are living for.

Whether you want to manifest the best table by the window at your favorite restaurant, some amazing seats in the front row of your upcoming conference, the most wonderful concert tickets of the season, or a new apartment that has an awesome ocean view, it doesn't matter the experience you are trying to have it's the journey that will take you there. All the things that you are wishing for or thinking of as a dream can be sent to the Universe and requested with affirmations and gratitude. If you maintain your positive thoughts, feelings, emotions, words, and visions, then your internal GPS will be able to keep your steps directed to the route that you need to reach those goals. Consider the way you clarify your goals, then direct your focus on the targeted vision that you have. You can accomplish these things with a vision board that is built for manifesting dreams.

- Be concise and clear about the purpose of your life.

Once there is a clear and concise idea of your targeted wish, then you will be able to stay focused and stay on track while working towards those goals. Your internal GPS will direct you where you need to go and the route you should take to get there. It will keep you on track and inform you when you are off track. Your happiness and joy over accomplishing your goals will lead you in the right direction. When you are properly aligned with your purpose, then you can truly begin to live your dream life.

When allowing the Universe to gift you with the goals that you wish to accomplish, then the powerful technology that the Universe is capable of utilizing is directed towards making your life much more magical. It's in these moments that you will find the magic as well as miracles that happen every day.

Consider what your lifestyle currently is like, and then examine these areas. What is your money status? How are the current relationships that you are in going to? In what way is your healthy supporting you?

Lastly, place all of your confidence in the fact that you will achieve whatever you wish to achieve. Imagine that your life was good, without complications, what would that look like to you? If money was not a concern, would you quit the job that you currently have? If the location was not a concern where would you be living? By regularly committing to practicing answering these questions, you will be able to have triggers that are powerful and invite manifestation of your wishes and dreams.

- Examine the passion that you hold.

This test developed by the Attwood's is called the examination of passion. It takes a deeper glance at what may well be an easy, as well as, elegant process to examine the passions that you have in your life. You will have to start by inputting the information into the form that is designed to ask questions such as: "When my life is true, I am ___." Fill in the blank spaces with random verbs to help you find the passions that you hold.

- Take time for yourself.

As we incline to look at our life a lot, it has become apparent that people often took extraordinarily little time for themselves. It is a constant complaint of those that are on call regularly, in meetings, scheduled to work extra shifts, and to cater to their needs at minimal capacity, that they lack in self-care. I have often asked myself why I do not take time for self-care, and the answer is simple. In order to live, you must work. Work takes president over health and self-care.

The problem then can become much clearer: By spending your entire life worried about work and not taking the time you need to tend to yourself, you will experience more stress, health issues, and even place yourself in line for an early death.

Rather than die myself, I would want to live a healthy and happy life. It does not pay off to kill myself with millions of to-dos that could be avoided or scheduled for later dates. This is why I commit to a self-care routine that helps me stay healthy and happy.

- Use your life purpose as well as passions to align with your goals

We measure our proficiency within life through the examination of our skills as well as, the interests that draw us to the purposes that we support in life. Once you take the time to acknowledge the purpose that you have in life, you can begin to organize those activities that you surround yourself with. Every step you take will be a reflection of the expression that shows your academic knowledge and your purpose. If the degree at which you perform your activities does not correspond appropriately with your goals, then your formula for success will not match up, and things will not work out. Take some time to align with your purpose so that your goals are proficiently set and then accomplished. You will have much more flexibility once you have an alignment of goals.

- Lean deeply into the life purpose that is true.

As soon as you are able to gain extra clarification around your purpose for life, you need to complete an overhaul of your life, and promptly start to live with purpose. By scheduling a life purpose plan, you can start to take systematic steps to reach your goals.

Live your daily life as if you are already living your purpose, then add in one single step each day to further your agenda. Consult with others about the feedback they can offer you about how they view you and whether or not they think you are living purposefully. Then compare the feedback with your own vision of how you are living.

# CHAPTER 25

# Heal and Build Self-Confidence

At some point in life our self-esteem declines because of procrastination. Procrastinating make our work mediocre and can tend to affect our performance in school, life, and work.

Building confidence come after the healing process. Confidence is a mysterious quality. It's one of those things we'd all like to have, but what does it really mean to be confident?

The problem with defining confidence as a feeling is that in practice it becomes a catch-22: If you don't feel confident, you're not likely to try.

There's another meaning of certainty, in spite of the fact that it's not as normal. The Latin foundations of certainty signify "with trust." Acting with trust ordinarily implies you're not totally sure of what you're doing—you're going out on a limb a. At the end of the day, it's our main thing that issues, less how we feel when we're doing it.

Where Confidence Comes From

Our convictions about ourselves are regularly formed by people around us, including family, companions, and media messages, sociologists have found. Yet, that doesn't mean your degree of certainty is out of your control—truth be told, it's an incredible opposite.

Certainty originates from being grounded in your feeling of self: recollecting what your identity is, the thing that you esteem, and the difficult work you've placed in.

Studies show that a straightforward idea exercise can assist individuals with diminishing their uneasiness in front of playing out an undertaking in a high-stakes circumstance. In explore drove by clinicians David Creswell and David Sherman, members were approached to pause for a minute to think about a basic belief—state, being an old buddy or regarding the earth. At that point, every individual expounded on a memory of a period they typified that esteem.

The individuals who did the activity had far lower adrenaline levels heading into unpleasant circumstances, for example, tests or open addresses, than the individuals who didn't—regardless of whether the guiding principle weren't at all applicable to the job needing to be done.

What made a difference was that the members were examining a profound truth about themselves, as opposed to an empty trademark, for example, "I'm the best."

An association with our true selves can likewise assist us with taking a portion of the weight off ourselves going into alarming circumstances. When Tanya was set to give a toast at her sister's wedding, she was phenomenally on edge about having everyone's eyes on her. She stressed over her hands shaking and her voice trembling. Be that as it may, when she considered it, intriguing every one of the 200 visitors with an impeccably conveyed discourse didn't genuinely make a difference to her. What was extremely critical to Tanya was giving her sister and new brother by marriage the amount she adored them and sought after their bliss. Considering that standard, she stood up at the service with for the most part quiet nerves and gave an ardent toast that reinforced the bonds she esteemed the most.

Obviously, not all self-question is an awful thing! Now and then dread is a sign that we haven't arranged enough for the huge introduction, the presentation, or the meeting. Rehearsing what you intend to state and do will give your brain something to swear by when the weight is high. The voice of self-uncertainty may likewise be stating we have to get more data, move in an alternate course, or enjoy a reprieve.

Be that as it may, we regularly decide in favor of dithering excessively. When you've placed in the long periods of training, you ought to have the option to make a move without fixating on what may turn out badly. We will give you the devices to change your mentality to a position of certainty. Building self-confidence is an ongoing process that needs determination and energy. Here are some steps to think about when you are trying to build yours:

Step 1: Step Out of Your Comfort Zone

If you are going to have unshakeable confidence, you have to be willing to step out of your comfort zone so that you can do things out of the ordinary. You have to stir up that urge burning within you to be extraordinary.

Perhaps you have a brilliant idea that your belief could benefit your company, but you do not know how to share that with your boss. Perhaps you have a crush that you never dared to approach.

The problem that comes with not acting on these desires is that you will stagnate right where you are. Truth is, when you fail to explore new experiences, you are letting fear take away your sunshine. You are simply digging deeper into your zone of comfort. The hole that you have been sitting in for several decades now.

Step 2: Know Your Worth

Did you know that people with rock solid confidence are often very decisive? One thing that is pretty admirable with successful people is that they do not take too much time trying to make small decisions. They simply do not overanalyze things. The reason why they can make fast decisions is that they already know their big picture, the ultimate outcome.

But how can you define what you want?

The very first step is for you to define your values. According to Tony Robbins, an author, there are two major distinct values; end values and means values. These two types of values are linked to the emotional state you desire; happiness, sense of security, and fulfillment among others.

Means Values

These simply refer to ways in which you can trigger the emotion you desire. A very good example is money, which often serves as a mean, not an end. It is one thing that will offer you financial freedom, something that you want and hence is a means value.

Ends Values

This refers to emotions that you are looking for, like love, happiness, and a sense of security. They are simply the things that your means values offer. For instance, the money will give you security and financial stability.

One way you can do that is ensuring that you define your end values. You can start by dedicating at least an hour or two each week to write down what your end values are. To get there, start by stating what your values are that you'd like to hone to get to your dream life.

Some of the questions that might help you put things into perspective include;

Step 3: Create your own happiness

Happiness is a choice, and also the best obstacles are self-generated constraints like thinking that you're unworthy of happiness.

If you do not feel worthy of joy, then you also don't believe you deserve the good things in life, the things that make you happy and that'll be precisely what keeps you from being happy.

You can be happier. It is dependent upon your selection of what you focus on. Thus, choose happiness.

Happiness is not something happens to you. It is a choice, but it takes effort. Don't wait for somebody else to make you happy because that may be an eternal wait. No external person or circumstance can make you happy.

Happiness is an inside emotion. External circumstances are responsible for just 10 percent of your happiness. The other 90% is how you behave in the face of those conditions and which attitude you adopt. The scientific recipe for happiness is external conditions 10%, genes 50 percent and intentional activities - that is where the learning and the exercises come in - 40%. Some people are born happier than others, but if you're born unhappier and practice the exercises, you will end up happier than somebody who had been born more joyful and does not do them. What both equations have in common is that the minimal influence of outside conditions on our happiness.

We usually assume that our situation has a much greater impact on our happiness. The interesting thing is that happiness is often found when you quit searching for it. Enjoy each and every moment. Expect miracles and opportunities at each corner, and sooner or later you will run into them. Whatever you focus on, you may see more of. Pick to concentrate on opportunities, decide to focus on the good, and choose to focus on happiness. Make your own happiness.

Step 4: Be Ready to Embrace Change

Have you ever found yourself obsessing about the future or the past? This is something that many of us find ourselves doing. However, here is the thing; the person you were five years ago or will be five years from now is very different from who you are right now.

You will notice that five years ago, your taste, interests, and friends were different from what they are today and chances are that they will be different five years from now. The point is, it is critical that you embrace who you are today and know that you are an active evolution.

According to research conducted by Carol Dweck, it is clear that children do well at school once they adopt a growth mindset. In fact, with the growth mindset, they believe that they can do well in a certain subject. This is quite the opposite of what children with a fixed mindset experience because they believe that what they are and all that they have is permanent. Therefore, having the notion that you cannot grow only limits your confidence.

What you should do to embrace all that you are is stopping self-judgment. Most of the time, we are out there, judging people by what they say, how they say it, what they wear, and their actions. In the same way, we judge ourselves in our heads comparing our past and present self.

For you to develop a strong sense of confidence, it is important that you start by beating the habit of self-judgment and negative criticism. Yes, this is something that can be difficult at first, but when you start to practice it, you realize how retrogressive that was.

You can start by choosing at least one or two days every week when you avoid making any judgment at all. If you have got nothing good to say, don't say it. If there is a negative thought that crosses your mind, you replace it with a positive one.

Gradually, your mind will start priming to a state of nonjudgment, and it will soon become your natural state of mind. This will not only help you embrace others but also accept yourself for who you truly are.

Step 5: Be Present

Sounds simple, right? It is important and necessary that you build your confidence. By being present, you are simply allowing your mind, body, and soul to be engaged in the task at hand.

Let us imagine speaking to someone that is not listening to what you are saying. This is something that has probably happened to a good number of us. How did you feel? On the other hand, imagine speaking to someone, and you feel like you were the only person in the room. Feels pretty special, huh?

The reason why you feel special is that they were present at that moment. They paid very close attention to what you were saying, feeling every emotion with you. They were engaged in the conversation at a deeper level. This way, you can retain information while still experiencing empathy.

To be present, you have to develop a mental double-check. This simply means that you should mentally check-in on yourself regularly. To do that, you have to develop a mental trigger or calendar when you ask yourself where your mind is. This is the time when you act as an observer of your mind.

Building confidence helps to avoid procrastination. High self-esteem means you're capable and confident of doing something.

# Conclusion

As we have discovered, procrastination is a learned activity. Procrastination is not a disease or something we are afflicted with. Procrastination is a behavior people do to avoid completing tasks. Procrastination causes dread and a person who is procrastinating actually feels like they have the weight of the world on their shoulders. This is not a great feeling and most people who procrastinate want desperately to learn how to do things in a more daily manner.

You can learn not to procrastinate. Remember, procrastination is expensive and costs more than just money. People have lost countless hours due to putting things off and waiting until the task at hand ending up costing twice as much money and three times the amount of time on the calendar. At this point, anything that costs extra money is just unacceptable. It's a wasteful expense to pay bills late and to have expenses compound because of items being put off until past the last minute.

Because of this and for other reasons, procrastination can ruin relationships as well. If you put off doing what you should do, in terms of safety and care for your family, that does not set well with a spouse when you have broken a trust.

Everything about your daily habits from diet and even exercise can affect the way you take on this behavior of procrastination. It all seems to come down to living in a more controllable manner where you are in control rather than being out of control. It is no fun to feel out of control. Feeling out of control is a feeling of powerlessness. You want to feel the power within and take charge of your life. By taking charge of your life, you can break the procrastination cycle no matter how it began.

Moreover, procrastination is an ever-growing problem in modern-day society, robbing countless people of the chance to achieve their ambitions and turn their dreams into reality. Many books have been written on the topic. However, most fail to address all of the causes of procrastination. As a result, they fall short when it comes to providing the tools needed to prevent procrastination, which is the critical first step toward conquering its effects in your life. Furthermore, they tend to only focus on the primary methods for overcoming procrastination, methods, which are useful, but not always the be-all and end-all.

Never forget that identifying the potential causes of procrastination is just the first step to becoming more productive and successful in life. The next step is to start taking charge of the situation at hand. There are two main things you need to take charge of in order to overcome laziness and procrastination once and for all. The first thing to take charge of is the project itself. All too often, people allow projects and tasks to control them when, in fact, it should be the other way around. Only when you take control of your actions can you take control of the direction your life takes. Therefore, it is critical that you take charge of every project you tackle in order to restore your sense of overall control. There are things that will reveal several ways in which you can take charge of any project, regardless of size and scope, and thus take control of your life overall.

Since procrastination is one of the main reasons why most people fail to achieve their goals in life, the ability to recognize and overcome it is absolutely vital if you hope to achieve any meaningful level of success. However, there are actually times when procrastination can be a useful tool, one which serves to teach lessons much the same way that failure does. Such lessons can include the notion that you are chasing the wrong dreams, that you are unprepared for the task at hand, or that you have given yourself too much to do. In this light, procrastination can actually help you to achieve your goals by revealing issues that need to be addressed before you can move forward. This will reveal some of the lesson's procrastination can teach along with how you can use those lessons to achieve the success you desire.

A lack of energy can cause a person to put off a project just as much as fear of failure or a confused mindset. That said, one way that you can prevent such physiological causes is to improve your physical health and wellbeing. The truth is that energy is the most vital element when it comes to achieving success in life. The more energy you have, the more effort you can invest in your goals and ambitions. Furthermore, increased energy has been shown to be a sure way for staving off such things as depression, laziness, and even confusion.

Motivation is another key factor when it comes to overcoming procrastination and achieving your goals. Unfortunately, many people suffer from a lack of motivation, making it easier to procrastinate and to put off the actions that would allow them to realize their dreams. The good thing is that motivation, like physical energy, can be nurtured and developed simply by practicing certain behaviors in your day-to-day life. By increasing your motivation, you will be able to overcome the temptation to procrastinate, making you more productive and successful as a result. There are more proven methods for getting back and maintaining motivation, thereby providing you with the tools needed to improve the quality of your life.

When you decide to do something, it can be hard to stick with it. This is especially the case where it's something that completely falls to you and no one else. In times like this, it's easy to get negative. If you let your mindset become a negative one, then you will find that you're constantly moving from bad situations to even worse ones. You can't focus. You can't think creatively. You have the energy for nada, and so nada is what you do.

While procrastination might be a sign that you have chosen a dream that is wrong for you in one way or another, it can also be a sign that the time is simply wrong for the goal you are pursuing. In this case, the dream can be the right one; it's just that you need more preparation before you can continue your journey. Rather than fighting and trying to overcome this type of procrastination, the trick is to use the delay to your advantage.

You have been acquired all the tools and insights you need in order to overcome the harmful effects of laziness and procrastination in your life and begin to pursue your dreams and ambitions, thereby living the life you truly deserve. The first thing you will be able to do now is to recognize all of the things that serve to create procrastination in the first place. This includes all of the negative people in your life, along with the pessimism and fear that they create in your mind due to their unfavorable outlook on life in general. Once you realize the harm that their words and attitudes have, you can protect yourself by limiting the amount of time you spend around such people. Not only will this protect your mind from unnecessary doubt and despair, it will also protect your vision for a happier, more satisfying life.

The most important thing is that you find what works for you. Different people will face different challenges in their life, meaning that no single solution will work for everyone. This has addressed so many different methods for overcoming procrastination. Additionally, it is focused on providing insights into laziness and procrastination. The more you understand the true nature of these things, the more capable you will be of not just overcoming them, but of mastering them on a whole new level. After all, procrastination can be a valuable ally in the pursuit of your dreams. Now that you understand both the negatives and the potential positives of procrastination you can own it in much the same way you can now own your projects, time, energy and even your dreams. Subsequently, nothing can stand in your way anymore when it comes to turning your dreams into reality. The very best of luck to you and your pursuit of success, your ambitions and the happiness you truly deserve!